BIGFOOT UNVEILED

SCIENTIFIC ANSWERS TO BIGFOOT MYSTERIES

RON MOREHEAD

CONTENTS

Rachelle Morehead Araque
1988–2020

This book is dedicated to
my beautiful daughter, Rachelle.

She piloted an airplane with me from Alaska to California, and as a SCUBA diver she dove with me among the Humboldt squid in the warm waters of Mexico.

I'm so proud of her and the grandchildren she brought me.

AL BERRY

Philosophy of Science

Science refers to a system of acquiring knowledge. Good science cannot be predicated on one's likes or dislikes, personal beliefs or disbeliefs, or unsupported whimsical assumptions—it has its disciplines.

Al Berry
(1941-2012)

DISCLAIMER

When reading this book, please keep in mind that much of my research led me to a theory that I am expressing. By all means, I don't think that I know everything as a fact. Several of these theories are based on other professional findings.

I don't claim to know what type of creature made the unusual vocalizations that we captured on cassette recorders in the high mountains of California. What I do know is that they left huge, five-toed impressions in the ground, and they have a vocal amplitude that can pierce a person to the core. We know that their unique vocal ability exceeds what a human can do; it signifies a complex language, and compared to humans, one of them represented a being over eight feet tall.[1] Rarely did we catch a glimpse of one, and when we did it was moving extremely fast. That said, because of their big foot impressions and their piercing voices, in this book, I'll refer to them (collectively) as Bigfoot with a capital B.

Since 1971, after interviewing many folks who have claimed encounters along with the scientific data that was obtained from the recorded interactions that my hunting friends and I captured, I have an educated idea as to what some of them may represent. That's right: some of them. I don't think they all have the same genetic code. The idea of a relic hominid that has been accepted by many researchers is not of the same type being that we encountered, but that is just my opinion. There may be some of the same genetic markers, but I've always had my doubts. This idea is primarily based upon the variances in the many foot impressions that have been cast by others elsewhere and in the many reports that I have heard regarding their appearance. Some have a sagittal crest, and some do not. If they were all from the same batch, that feature should be shared (dilution from crossbreeding factor exempt, which will be discussed later in a chapter about Hybridization).

However, in order to consider my thoughts, it will require a paradigm that is not fixated, one that does not have a preconceived idea of what they are. Yes, a lot of people think they know. But the difference here is not just because I have been researching so long, but because I've experienced them on several occasions, over several years, and listened to many others who have claimed an encounter.

As my fifty-plus years of researching the Bigfoot

phenomena progresses, my thoughts about these creatures can and do change, too. The ones that the other hunters and I dealt with at the Sierra Camp are either completely alien or part human and part something else. However, I believe many of these hairy giants are hybrids that can reproduce with humans, so they would have twenty-three pairs of chromosomes.

Humans are alive on this planet for an average of around eighty years and tend to not understand just how long other inhabitants have been here—some human and some not. I think we need to better understand the big picture, not just what Bigfoot could be, but what their intentions might be. Why haven't we found one? Why are they so elusive? Often their intent may appear to be friendly and virtuous, but hold on, take a deep breath, read some history, and remember: a parachute only works when it opens.

In this book it may seem that I sway at times from the Bigfoot topic and drift into my ideas of life itself and quote ancient texts. What is life on this planet is meant to be, and just how do Bigfoots play a role in this picture? Many, if not all, are humanlike and have sapience, so do they have the same abilities that we have? Could they have more abilities than we do?

ACKNOWLEDGMENTS

This book has taken me a lot longer to write than it may have taken a real writer. Without the willingness of Keri Campbell, my beloved, to help with correction and to help get me out of the trees so I could see the forest, it would have taken longer.

In addition to Keri's input, I have quoted several physicists and also delved deeper into ancient texts and Native American mythology to find common denominators that fit with my persuasion, so I have a big "Thank you" to all those who grabbed hold of my attention and caused me to step a little further into this quantum arena. My special thanks to Dr. Paul Dirac, Albert Einstein, Nikola Tesla, Stephen Hawking, Michio Kaku, Paul Planck, Erwin Schrödinger, Sir Isaac Newton, Richard Feynman, and a host of others.

My special thanks to Beth Wojiski for her help with this book, and a big thanks to artist Dan Cassity for his excellent illustration of a Bigfoot face, which he made for the cover.

STATEMENT BY
CHRISTOPHER MURPHY
AUTHOR AND PREEMINENT CANADIAN
BIGFOOT AUTHORITY

"My entrance into this discipline was essentially occasioned by Ron Morehead and his book, *The Quantum Bigfoot* (2017). Ron explored things from both a biblical/religious perspective and as a result of his own experiences. Ron is considered one of the most important researchers in hominology, so I take him very seriously. I have expanded on his material and provided my own conclusions. Please don't confuse what we both say, although I believe we are similar."

FOREWORD BY DAVID PAULIDES

The Bigfoot and UFO worlds are filled with people claiming to be experts, experiencers, and researchers. The majority of the "experts" believe Bigfoot is an ape, with the predominant belief that it is *Gigantopithecus*. This animal has been extinct for 350,000 years, with no physical evidence of it ever being in North America. Only a small handful of researchers have challenged the *Gigantopithecus* finding. You are about to read an eloquent overview of Bigfoot that will set history straight.

I first met Ron Morehead at a Bigfoot conference after listening to the Sierra Sounds. The language Ron recorded at the Sierra Camp is not just unique; it shatters many standard science teachings. Many years later and more bigfoot conferences than I care to remember, I approached Ron after we had both given our presentations, and I asked if I could come to his

Sierra Camp for a week and record his story. Thankfully, Ron said yes.

I think that we would all agree that you don't really know someone until you live with them. Well, me, Ron, Scott Nelson, and my videographer spent eight days at the Sierra Camp—days I will never forget. Nothing paranormal happened, but I had one of the great gifts of my lifetime. I got to know Mr. Morehead at an entirely different level. We spent countless hours over the fire talking, sharing ideas, laughing, and experiencing one of life's great treats: a Ron Morehead-cooked breakfast! Bar-non, Ron is the Wolfgang Puck around the campfire!

In this book, Ron takes you through his life: flying his plane, riding his horse, and escaping to his hunting camp. He explains the Paracas skull DNA and Dr Ketchum's Bigfoot findings and walks you through the delicate explanation of Quantum Physics and its relationship to the hairy biped.

Ron and I have spent decades running a parallel research path on the topic of Bigfoot. The findings you will read are factual, thoroughly researched, have a scientific foundation, and have been withheld by every cable television show. Mr. Morehead is a groundbreaker in Bigfoot research through his innovative and successful approaches to complex issues.

Lastly, I lost my son Ben a short time ago, the biggest emotional blow in my life, nothing comes close. Around this same time, Ron lost his beautiful daughter Rachelle, to which this book is dedicated.

Soon after these events, I saw Ron at a conference, gave him a huge hug, and had tears in my eyes. I felt sad for Ron, simultaneously thinking of Ben and Rachelle. Ron hugged me and said God has them in a good place; they knew we loved them.

Ron's words were comforting and gentle, and he obviously cared for my mental health, but that is Ron Morehead. A caring, introspective soul gifted with the ability to conduct significant research, pen riveting books, and live a life we all wish we had experienced.

Congratulations, Ron, on a great book!

I love you, Brother.

—David Paulides
Missing 411

INTRODUCTION
WHY ANOTHER BOOK?

It began with a sleepless night. I've found that those kinds of nights can often have a unique meaning; however, sometimes it's just a matter of too much caffeine. But on this night, caffeine wasn't the problem. How do I more clearly explain the enigmas that I and so many others have experienced (or at least claim to have experienced)? But I think more important is the "why" it's happening and my thoughts about all that. Those thoughts rang just underneath my scalp and above my pillow—no sleep.

Important questions were often answered for Nikola Tesla after he awoke from sleeping. However, many questions loomed in my mind, so I needed (I thought) to write another book. After all, I think that I know more now than I did before . . . more quantum ideas to capture for those who understood my previous book, *Quantum Bigfoot*. I think the evidence that I now have is very suggestive, if not undeniable, that the sounds we captured in the Sierras represents a unique complex language. It's important to understand how our unusual human attributes actually came about (e.g., telepathy, consciousness, etc.). It could give us a better idea on many of the characteristics of Bigfoot.

To capture the demographic that I think I should have and hold the reader's attention, the book ought to have the word "Bigfoot" placed on the cover, which begat my title, *Bigfoot Unveiled*. After all there were some very unusual enigmas associated with the beings we encountered in those high mountains of California, and although my research into the laws of physics answers some, many questions still linger in the ether.

After writing *The Quantum Bigfoot*, I thought I was finished. But still too many strange things being reported, unanswered by classical science and mainstream researchers, were not taking hold of some of this author's ideas; they are still looking for the ape in the woods. That's understandable because many of the features reported by witnesses say they resemble a great ape. The other hunters, who I was with thought the same. But the strangeness we began experiencing stumped all of us.

Years ago, quantum science had captured my interest and wouldn't let go. Rather than ignore that science, I embraced it. Now I find myself with the need to expand and bring more to the readers' consideration. I am compelled to try and explain the bigger picture, where the dots are leading me.

My desire in life was (and still is) not to write, but to learn more. When I was a child, I always looked at the night sky and wondered, "Where is the end of space?" Nobody could answer that question for me, so there I was growing up wondering how space could end. Newtonian rules are based on everything being measurable and predictable. Later in life, when I asked a group of academics how far it is to the end of the universe, I got taken off their email list. But now my answer has arrived: the cosmos can't have an end. It must be conceived, but never actually totally understood using our mostly accepted human construct. That human attribute keeps us trapped in an environment of having to just believe that the cosmos has no end but never understanding it. For physicists, the equations in quantum physics can be understood, but what those equations represent cannot always be seen. It begins in the microworld of unseen electrons and positrons, which move in an energetic matter. Some say that it only works in the microworld (e.g., microwave ovens, cell phones, etc.) but that always puts a "bump" in my brain processor. If it is a law in physics, then it is a law that must work everywhere.

Finally, I ran across a professor, Dr. Christopher Baird at West Texas A&M, who states that all things, from the atom to the stars, work under the laws of quantum physics.[1] His article made me feel a lot better. It seems that unless there is a professor who states this stuff, it is not accepted by a lot of people, and I'm not a professor, just an open-minded citizen scientist who thinks that all questions must have an answer.

If you don't have an open mind, you'll get lost in the weeds of classical science (like Newtonian physics from 1687) and start accepting everything that is taught, never questioning much. Max Planck, the father of quantum mechanics who won the Nobel Prize in 1918, knew that the standard classical physics model just didn't answer how all things work. He got the quantum ball rolling, though, which opened up a way through mathematics that helps with the answers to how all things work, not just the seen but also the unseen.

Can we believe in things that we cannot witness? Can we understand that there's no end to the cosmos when we certainly do not see one? Yet, Newtonian physics claims everything is measurable, and yes, everything in our 3D environment is. But no, not everything is measurable. We were conditioned to embrace what our fifth-grade teacher taught us, right? No, we shouldn't . . . not everything. Many enigmas are experienced around Bigfoot, and I am going to write about some of them while at the same time do my best to give a reasonable, understandable explanation as to how they may have happened. Not just that, but how the puzzle seems to be coming together for a picture of why it's all happening.

My first book, *Voices in the Wilderness*, is my forty-five-year chronicle of some of what went on with me and my hunting friends at that wilderness camp during the early 1970s. I tried to explain some of those strange happenings detailed in that first book. In my second book, *The Quantum Bigfoot*, the subtitle of which is "Bringing Science and Spirituality Together." Why? Because I found that Tesla, Einstein, and other physicists studied the Veda, but also, I was raised in a Christian environment and studied ancient texts like the bible and Greek mythology. I thought they were very interesting, religion and science on the same page. No, but spirituality and quantum science are on the same page!

"Science without religion is lame, religion without science is blind" Albert Einstein.

I think if Einstein could have said that a few years later, he would have replaced the word *religion* with *spirituality*. What is spirituality, anyway, and what does it have to do with Bigfoot?

Okay, when I first introduced my quantum book, many people began to call me a woo-wooer, insinuating that I was a paranormal researcher. At first, I thought that was a bit rude because paranormal research and quantum science are not the same, although quantum science can and does explain many things that are reported as paranormal—there's an answer for everything. Nikola Tesla said, "What one man calls God, another calls the laws of physics."[2]

So I say if you believe in the pearly gates, heaven, or any type of life after death, you might be in the same camp with me. If you go to church or synagogue on Sunday, give an offering, and pray to God, Buddha, or the Universe, you are probably a person who wants to do the right thing. I stopped going to church and do not consider myself a religious person. Religions often get caught in a trap of thinking they have the only answers to life and the afterlife, and it typically comes with a strong dose of judgment against those not of the same faith.

So let it be said that I am a citizen scientist who studies the macro- and microworld of physics: bring that paranormal stuff on and allow me to offer a scientific explanation based on the rules of quantum physics. After that I will offer my idealistic view of what all this may mean.

A MISUSE OF RESEARCH

My research into the Bigfoot phenomena spans over fifty years. My first book, *Voices in the Wilderness*, was my chronicle of encounters with Bigfoot that my hunting friends and I had while at our hunting camp in the remote Sierra Nevada mountains of California in the 1970s. My second book, *The Quantum Bigfoot*, which melds science and spirituality, came a few years later. This is my third book.

My good friend Alan Berry (1941–2012) encouraged me to begin writing about the events at the Sierra Camp which began for me in 1971. Al was an investigative reporter working for a newspaper in Redding, California. He had been contacted by the late Peter Byrne, a big game hunter whose colorful history included leading several safaris into Nepal. At that time, Peter had a Bigfoot research outpost in Oregon.

He had been contacted by Ivan Sanderson, a cryptozo-ologist, who had received a twenty-three-page hand-written letter from Warren Johnson, the leader of our hunting group at the Sierra Camp. That letter, which was not considered credible at the time, had been passed on to Mr. Byrne, who also considered it a prob-able hoax. I didn't know those men considered the story a hoax until years later when I read the corre-spondence from Al Berry's files. These types of inter-actions have never been reported before.

We took Al Berry into our camp in 1972. Besides being an investigative reporter, he had been an officer in the Army who saw action in Vietnam and was also a good, straightforward writer. We eventually became good friends and began to travel to different meets to present the sounds that we had all recorded. It seems, however, that the evidence we'd collected and the happenings that surrounded the camp were too much for most to accept as true. Therefore, the only time we discussed the unusual stuff was with our family and close friends, not with the general public. Al had two degrees in science, one a masters, and presenting that unusual stuff was not sitting well with him; although he wrote a small part of it in a book with B. Ann Slate, called *Bigfoot* (a Bantam book published in 1978) describing orbs that the Johnson brothers reported as following them around. The Johnsons began hunting that area in 1958.

With Al's encouragement, I began to write about my experiences with the Bigfoot phenomenon; the first book was my chronicle that began in 1971. However, as rare as repeated encounters are, it was considered by some scientists to be an abomination to the subject: a misuse of research. These beings, if they exist, must be an undiscovered great ape. I believe that they prematurely arrived at that because of their fixed discipline of classical science. If anything exists it must conform to those parameters; otherwise, it doesn't exist. After all, within the box of classical sciences, everything is measurable and predictable. So how could something such as Bigfoot be anything other than what classical science suggests; in other words, flesh and blood only, a relic hominid who has evolved through the eons of time? I say maybe some of them are just that. But because of our experiences up in the Sierras, I think a deeper look is in order.

In order to learn something new, our mind must be open to new data yet still remain objective. Those who disagree with the idea that Bigfoot is anything other than a flesh-and-blood creature tend to judge those who have witnessed something outside their personal paradigm. So is anything actually paranormal, or is it perhaps something just waiting to be understood?

For years I have thought that if a rule in science is established anywhere, it must be everywhere. If the quantum laws existing in the microworld are true, they would have to be true in our macroworld also. According to modern science, quantum physics is how everything in the cosmos actually works, so I'm right.

"In reality, every object in the universe (from atoms to stars) operates according to quantum physics."[1]

Christopher Baird, Physicist, West Texas A & M.

Over my five decades of research, I have been accused of promoting illogical, irrational, nonsensical stuff and using my experiences to cause people to get delusional. But having interacted with these beings' multiple times, I know of no scientist who has had any direct experience with them as I have. I doubt if any have even read my second book, *The Quantum Bigfoot*, or reviewed the complimentary download I offered them. I think all scientists should consider this alternative view of their classical teachings.

The late astronaut Dr. Edgar Mitchell said "It takes classical and quantum sciences together to have a clear perception." So why don't classical scientists get on board with how things actually work on this planet? Could it disturb their comfort zone? With respect to those who spent many hours burning the midnight oil to get through the next days' test, and afterward spending years paying back their student loans, I can understand. However, the truth must come out at some point, and you would think that those who consider it is possible for Bigfoot to exist would question me, or perhaps question one or two of the other guys involved with me at that camp, while some of us are still upright.

Dr. Edgar Mitchell, Astronaut

My interactions with these beings led me to understand that what the other hunters and I dealt with in the Sierras can do things that are outside of our normal understanding. That's what brought me to quantum physics: a possible "scientific" explanation to some of the mysteries that are associated with these beings and are very often reported by others who have experienced them too.

So I really don't care if some people think it's a misuse of research. There are many people now who are coming forth and reporting some of the same things that we experienced at that camp. Of course, not all who have witnessed a Bigfoot have unusual things happen.

That said, I have reason to believe that the beings referenced as Bigfoot or Sasquatch are not of the same genome, and I write about that in this book. I also bring up the probability of an alien connection.

The veil that I am partly seeing through is getting thinner, and hopefully many of the readers of this book will also get a glimpse—especially those who think that my work is a misuse of research.

2

BODY AND SOUL

The way that I believe classical physics and modern physics combine for all of humanity's embodiments, and possibly Bigfoot too, is simple. We all have two components in our bodies: physical and ethereal. Our brain is part of the physical; brought about by evolution, it controls bodily functions. The inner attribute, our consciousness, is the ethereal, spiritual, energetic soul, put into our DNA by high frequency beings. (The plural part of *beings* is explained in chapter 6.)

According to Einstein, "Energy cannot be created or destroyed, it can only be changed from one form to another."[1] It gives us our intuitiveness, our feelings, and other great abilities. Energy is the ethereal part of our embodiment . . . our soul, our spirit, placed within our physical body by God. That said, we are privileged to enjoy these two elements together, but rarely do humans understand how this works. Most of us believe that we are just a body and subject to what the day brings: here today and perhaps tomorrow.

Thanks to Darwin for his pursuit of how different species evolved on this planet. Classical science has adopted his theory on how, from the most minute level out of the ocean, we evolved into a primate. I don't argue with that theory, except for the "we" part, but how did Bigfoot evolve and how did consciousness evolve—or did it actually evolve? Most of us have had unusual experiences that we've wondered about. For instance, if we have been thinking about a person, and then the phone rings and it is that person. Or we've had a feeling about something and end up very happy we followed that feeling because it led to something good. But many times our conditioned, analytical mind will talk us out of how we actually felt about something.

In recent times I have continually heard that our brain and heart need to be in coherence or rhythmically balanced. I totally agree; however, it seems to me that the heart must get the information from another source, I think the pineal gland, which is a small gland inside of our brain…is our receiver. But where does it get its information? My thought is that all three of these components must be communicating with each other as one. Our pineal gland receives from a higher energetic frequency, which knows what is right or wrong for us; then our heart (gut feeling) gets it and sends it to the brain, which should follow that message. Much too often, however, our brain analyzes that feeling and goes a different way, and many times the analyzing takes a long time, and often it takes us in the wrong direction—and that puts a wedge in our Oneness, which we're here to develop. From birth, each person has been conditioned with the information that he or she has been taught.

We cannot deny that the troglodytes (cavemen) were here, but I personally don't think they had the same attributes that we humans ended with.

I believe that advance energic aliens messed with the ancient man's DNA, for debatably different reasons. Afterward, however, I think the caveman was messed with again. Those alien beings did not get what they previously intended, so there was another upgrade, and that's who we are. They wanted a hominid to be like them. As is said in Genesis 1:26: "Let us make man in our image."

In my opinion these beings from the cosmos made Bigfoot by altering the DNA of a primate. Eons later, they also made *Homo sapiens sapiens*.

What should we call these high-frequency beings? The Fallen Ones, an alien, or perhaps the Anunnaki. I believe there could be millions of these types of aliens in the universe, some of them good. And then there are some that decided to not be good, using their free will to go against a mandate to not interfere with humans. But here we are, being interfered with.

That said, there's an alternative idea, which many ascribe to and should be considered. Bigfoot might be of a completely different genome, a being that came here from somewhere in the cosmos for reasons unknown.

The third idea is that they must be a relic hominid and their bodies evolved to adapt naturally. However, science says that energy cannot die, and everything is energy, suggesting that Bigfoot, whatever they are, must possess something besides just flesh and blood.

3

WHERE'S THE PROOF?

Alan Berry, the investigative reporter who we took into the Sierra Camp in 1972, worked diligently to get academia to prove or disprove the sounds that he'd captured at the Sierra Camp. He wanted to find an expert who would give an unbiased study of what he'd captured. All of us took our cassette recorders to that camp, so there were certainly a lot of redundant cassette recordings of these beings' chatter. However, Al, being the professional that he was, knew to use only new, fresh, cassette tapes. He also knew that in order to have those tapes analyzed it was important they not be compromised in any way. Most of us would take our recordings home and transfer them to a reel-to-reel, which would hold a lot of stuff, and then reuse the cassette on the next trip.

Anticipating that Bigfoot might come around that

evening, Al would start his recorder and wait. Therefore he captured some of the vocalizations from beginning to end. The rest of us usually waited until we
heard something to suggest one of these beings was
around and then started our recorders; that is not a
good way to do it.

After a couple of years of going to the camp, Al
had exhausted all avenues of this being a possible
hoax. When the winter snow kept us out, he took his
recordings and began to solicit academia. He went to
the best that he could find, who would take on the
task of analyzing what he'd captured. He had a
master's degree in science and understood what any
serious scientist would need.

The following is a statement that he wrote
regarding his efforts to obtain help:

I pursued the matter to an end in 1978, when Dr. R.
Lynn Kirlin, then at the University of Wyoming, and
a Norwegian graduate student of electrical engineering, Lasse Hertel, presented their findings of the
sound recordings at a University of British
Columbia symposium entitled "Anthropology of the
Unknown."[1]

By this time, I had taken a fair amount of ridicule
and scorn from the academic community in an effort
to enlist scientific interest. At least one prominent
scientist, Dr. Phillip Lieberman, then of the University of Connecticut, who is an expert in primate
vocalization, at least of the Rhesus monkey, at first

offered help then accused me of being a former student whom he had flunked and was trying to discredit him. Another PhD on the West Coast whom Kirlin referred me to used the recordings in his classroom as an example of how clever people can be when it comes to hoaxing others. His name was Minifie, University of Washington, as I recall. I have no quarrel with these folks, really.[2]

As history would have it, the following are some of the results from people who took their scientific research seriously and put their academic colleague's criticism on the back burner. However, the previous statement by Al shows some of what he went through with those who were more interested in their career than expanding scientific knowledge. It seems most in the scientific community took this subject matter as a joke. More often than not, the "joke" problem still exists today. Thankfully, as the years go by, this is beginning to change.

Prior to Dr. Kirlin's year-long analysis, Syntonic Research, based in New York, listened to the recordings. This is the firm that analyzed the Watergate tapes by President Nixon. Because they heard no sixty-cycle hum, which would have immediately shown that the tapes were prerecorded and also suggested that the voices on the tapes were too powerful for the human voice, they took the sounds seriously. They suggested that Al find an academic sound engineer who would take on the task at no expense. His complete collaborative notes to the president of Syntonic, I. E. Teibel, are in the back of a book that he coauthored with B. Ann Slate, *Bigfoot*, published by Bantam Press in 1976. Although Al knew that what he and the rest of us had captured could be groundbreaking, he also knew that the first issue was to find a professional sound engineer, someone with a PhD, to verify (or not) that the tapes were not manipulated in any way.

There is a term called *cognitive dissonance* that Al ran into many times, and some people carry it with them forever. They'll say something like "Don't confuse me with the facts. I've made up my mind."

According to the Simply Psychology website, cognitive dissonance "refers to a situation involving conflicting attitudes, beliefs, or behaviors. This produces a feeling of mental discomfort leading to an alteration in one of the attitudes, beliefs, or behaviors to reduce the discomfort and restore balance."[3]

The Facts

Although some of these facts were covered in *The Quantum Bigfoot*, I will reiterate some of them here and also add a statement by Dr. Lieberman, a cognitive language professor from Brown University who's research seems to confirm to me that these beings must have a human component.

Dr. R. Lynn Kirlin, Professor Emeritus – University of Wyoming

In 1978 after a year-long study by Dr. Lynn Kirlin, professor of electrical engineering at the University of Wyoming, and his student Lasse Hertel, wrote a professional paper that showed that there was no evidence of the Sierra recordings having been manipulated in any  way. They were not sped up, slowed down, and there was no sixty-cycle hum—all signs of manipulated audio.

He could detect no deception in those cassette tapes and concluded the sounds were made at the time of recording. Many of the frequencies go beyond what the average human can do and represent a being eight feet, two inches tall by their vocal pitch (compared to humans), and seven feet, four inches tall by their vocal tract length.[4]

In *Manlike Monsters on Trial*, Dr. Kirlin said of the tapes "If Bigfoot is actually proven to exist, the vocalizations on these tapes may well be of great anthropological value, being a unique observance of the Bigfoot in his natural environment."

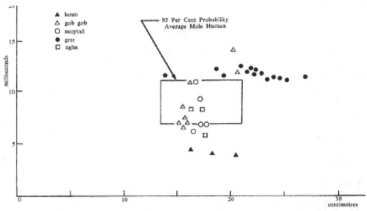

FIGURE 4. PITCH AND VOCAL TRACT LENGTH ESTIMATES WITH APPROXIMATE 95 PER CENT PROBABILITY REGION FOR NORMAL HUMAN MALE SUPERIMPOSED

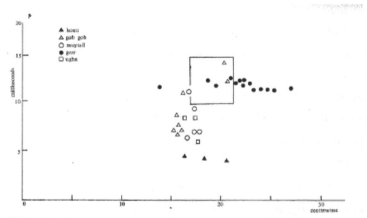

FIGURE 5: SAME DATA AS IN FIGURE 4, BUT 95 PER CENT PROBABILITY CORRESPONDS TO LOW-PITCHED HUMAN MALE AND THE VOWEL 3 WHICH REQUIRES A LONG TRACT LENGTH

Scott Nelson was a career cryptolinguist with the Navy and is a two-time graduate of the Defense Language Institute of Foreign Language Center in

Monterey, California, which is one of the largest language schools in the world.

Mr. Nelson's career in the Navy was to collect and intercept foreign messages and determine whether or not the message was a code or a language and, if it was a language, to determine whether there were any signs of deception in that language. After a long study,

Scott Nelson,
Cryptolinguist, US Navy

he found no deception in the Sierra recordings and also wrote a transcription code for researchers to use for analyzing captured vocalizations. He also determined that the Sierra Giants have a complex language by the human definition of language: a stream of words that make up a sapient sentence. He also stated that the vocalizations could not be duplicated by the human vocal mechanism.

Scott Nelson's schooling in cryptolinguistics was vetted by J. Edward Boring, chief knowledge officer at the Defense Language Institute Foreign Language Center (DLIFLC). The entire letter can be read in my previous book, *"The Quantum Bigfoot."*

Dr. Philip Lieberman – Fred M. Seed Professor of Cognitive and Linguistic Sciences and Department of Anthropology, Brown University.

The focus of Dr. Lieberman's research was the evolution of the biological bases of human language and cognition. This includes both the specialized anatomy necessary to produce articulate speech and the neural circuits that confer the reiterative ability that enables humans to produce a potentially infinite number of sentences from a finite number of elements. Dr. Lieberman stated that only humans have the vocal mechanism for cognitive speech (language). No other animal on this planet has that capability.

It's interesting that this statement was made by one of the professors who thought Al Berry was a former student trying to discredit him, which he was not.

Dr. Melba Ketchum – Geneticist, Sasquatch Genome Project

A Five-Year Genome Study AT DNA Diagnostics Yields Evidence of Homo sapiens/Unknown Hominin Hybrid Species in North America. Dallas, TX (PRWEB) November 24, 2012.

For many years, because I knew the integrity of many people involved with Dr. Ketchum's study, I thought that her professional analysis would knock the wonderment ball out of the Bigfoot ballpark—a breaking point for the Bigfoot community. Instead, many who are on the Bigfoot circuit gave her study two thumbs down. I had a difficult time understanding why any professional or presenter in this field would do that to anyone (even if they thought it), especially when it can damage the career of the individual—someone who also spent years getting an education plus years of training to obtain credentials to do that type of work.

When conference speakers are asked about that study, they feel pressure to make a statement, so they follow the leader who has the clout to sway the layman. More often than not, their statement is negative when asked about Dr. Ketchum's project. They want to stay with classical reasoning (i.e., academia's parameters). That narrow thinking, in my opinion, will never provide a forward outcome. Their scientific teachings say that if the sample is not in the worldwide gene banks, it just can't exist; therefore, the sample must be contaminated by a human interference.

A book written by the late Scott Carpenter, called *Truth Denied, The Sasquatch DNA Study*, is a good place to review the chronicle of Dr. Ketchum's work and the fallout that came afterward. Aside from her scientific findings, Dr. Ketchum commented on how the human component may have been introduced into the specimens that she had. By looking into ancient texts and the giants mentioned in those writings, it may have been received negatively by academia given her opinion fell outside of the acceptable practice of science these days. In those writings alien beings (falling angels) altered the DNA of the troglodytes, thus introducing giants and corrupting the human genome. Most of us believe that over eons different types of aliens have visited this planet. I have personally seen evidence of advanced technology in South America.

I think many on both sides of this Bigfoot fence are reevaluating her findings and comments now that our government has acknowledged that UFO/UAP (Unidentified Aerial Phenomena) and aliens are real. People are opening their minds to a possible contact. Our government is allowing many of the individuals who covertly worked on alien craft to speak about it now. Then, of course, there's the Space Force which was created for a reason: supposedly for our protection. More on this subject can be found in chapter 9, Hybridization.

To recap the above, is the jury still out? Let's review:

1. Dr. Kirlin said there was no manipulation to the recordings, which represent an animal eight feet tall.
2. Scott Nelson said what was recorded is a complex language and that there was no evidence of manipulation to the recordings. He also said that human voices cannot duplicate all those vocalizations.
3. Dr. Lieberman said that only humans have cognitive speech (language).
4. Dr. Ketchum found the human genome in her DNA study of evidence collected from researchers of these beings.

These people are professionals, and their credibility is based on their credentials and track record. Anyone who chooses to believe that these professionals are correct should come to this conclusion because it is a simple deduction: the recordings represent a language, and only humans have a capability for language, yet many of the vocalizations from the beings recorded are outside the human range, as is their average size. Therefore, these beings, who we call Bigfoot or Sasquatch, must have a human component; a hybrid being—like us but not exactly.

Many of you may have read my last book, *The Quantum Bigfoot*. If so, you know that I believe, as do theoretical physicists, that all things throughout the universe work within the rules of quantum physics and are not limited by the laws of three-dimensional Newtonian physics.

None of us would go bear hunting with a stick, try to hold a tiger by a string or hunt fish with a squirt gun. This is how I consider those Bigfoot researchers who search for these giants using the restricted laws of Newtonian physics only, when quantum physics is another tool at their disposal. That said, however, I understand their position. I was also in that camp years ago; it's how I was taught and did not know about, or understand, quantum physics when I entered this field of Bigfootology.

I do, however, consider most of those researchers my friends, and I certainly do not look down on them. They are using the only method that they have been conditioned in. I only want to help by using my first-hand experiences and endless hours of self-study in the field of modern physics, especially how it possibly relates to Bigfoot and humans alike.

So, without harvesting a body but having presented my data in this chapter with professional documentation, I'm hopeful that more will consider this proof enough to change the minds of the scientific world.

However, let's look at this from another angle. What would happen if someone did get the data that academia would consider enough to declare what many of us think we know? What would our government be forced to do? That question should give us all something to consider. History books would need to be changed worldwide; we would need to know how many of these giants are existing, and their habitat, like: How is that even possible? How much land would need to be put aside as their habitat? And other questions naturally follow.

Let's face it: Our government does know about these creatures but doesn't know how to control the greater knowing. And if they do not know how to control it, they hide it or discredit it. Perhaps at some point in the future researchers will supply academia with enough data that they will be forced to acknowledge these entities exist. Then, of course, our lawmakers would appropriate a few billion dollars for a useless study.

Like us, in my opinion, many of these beings are sapient and did not evolve all of their abilities naturally. A physical body may have evolved, perhaps like the Gigantopithecus, but their sentiency came through an alteration in their genetics by a type, or types, of technologically advanced "something(s)" into a primate. Our physical bodies evolved over eons, too (as in the troglodytes), but several thousands of years ago the DNA changed to become *Homo sapiens sapiens*, and we came to know right from wrong. We were endowed with a special "oneness," a connection to the image of very high-frequential beings with the knowledge of the universe—in other words: God, cognizance. However, we regressed from that oneness and need to evolve over again (i.e., change back). As in the good book, "Be born again." (John 3:7 KJV)

Bigfoot has cognizance and in some ways are humanlike but they are definitely not like us. As I've said many times, they are bigger, stronger, faster, and extremely stealthy. How they evolved some of those unique attributes is one of the things we want to learn. Some say they just evolved naturally, nothing but flesh and blood, and others say that there is an alien connection, and they are interdimensional.

There have been hundreds of UFO/UAP accounts that suggest that these creatures may have a shared connection. As in ancient traditions, in biblical history, and in Greek mythology, aliens have been here and have reproduced with human women, creating a hybrid of gigantic stature. This planet is the jewel of our solar system, and they would love to have what humans have been given: dominion. But we are not doing a good job of taking care of it.

Over eons of time, and because I believe that many Native American legends started with a core of truth, I think that some Bigfoot beings have crossbred with indigenous people; thus, some have more humanlike characteristics than others. Some can do what others cannot.

On my second CD, I encouraged developing a trust relationship with these creatures. There are ones that appear to want to befriend us; there are ones that do not want anything to do with us; and according to the Paiutes in Nevada, who claim to have warred with cannibalistic, red-haired giants, some might abduct us for a tasty snack. Then there's Portlock, Alaska, currently a ghost town, where it has been recorded that a giantlike being, who they called Nantinaq, killed and mangled over thirty villagers. Fearing for their lives, the inhabitants abandoned the village in the late 1940s.

We humans tend to live in a one-hundred-year bubble; our lifespan was shortened a few thousand years ago, so we do not live as long as we used to. I encourage people to understand what all this could mean in terms of this planet's big picture. Combine this with the giants that are here now and be cautiously aware of what they might be here for. My advice is that anyone encountering these beings should do your best to control your fear. Keep your guard up, but most of all know that you as a human are special: you have been given dominion on this planet by high-frequency beings and were not short-changed in terms of attributes. It doesn't get any better than that; we can all reclaim what we were originally designed for. We will find all the connection needed within us—it just takes being still and flowing with that universal consciousness that we are all part of. By paying attention to that inner voice, you can be led into all that is right for you. Honor your feelings, not your fears. We must, however, make sure our brain, heart, and pineal gland are all in sync.

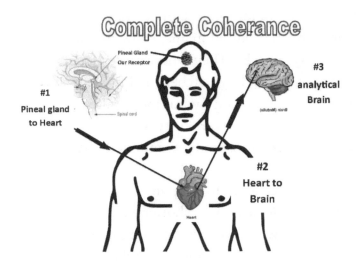

4

AN APE IN THE WOODS

I n 1971, when I first heard about the Johnson brothers' encounter and was asked by Donald to join him to see if the other hunters were okay (they were late coming out), I was on board. I'd heard the story about a type of monster that they had encountered at the Sierra Camp, so I made that imposing eight-mile hike. Donald didn't tell me how hard it would be. I did not give a thought to what these giants could be, other than an undiscovered animal . . . assuming they even existed. I knew the men involved, and their integrity was impeccable. So I figured something unique was fixing to be part of my life; I just didn't know or have any idea how exceptional or how important it would become.

The existence of these beings in modern times was in opposition to my upbringing. Having been conditioned in Christianity and still going to church, I was on the edge, thinking about the biblical giants like the Nephilim and fallen angels. Surely they couldn't still be around, but if they were, this trip could get really bad.

A lot of researchers and witnesses claim negative encounters, but as far as I know, no one has recently been attacked or killed. Of course, people go missing quite regularly, but nothing is sure unless they return or the body is found. We have that historical report from over seventy years ago that came out of Portlock, Alaska, where several mangled and dead villagers were found. It was claimed a giant, Bigfootlike creature was responsible. I went there in 2021 with a production company that worked with the heirs of Portlock to hopefully reestablish their abandoned fishing village. They said they wanted someone to let them know if it was safe to do so—no pressure on me at all.

What is safe? If these beings are just another ape running around killing people, then NO . . . it's not safe. However, after evaluating the Portlock area from a helicopter, seeing previous timbering from decades ago, and listening to the stories that were written about that village, I had an idea that could be helpful. I mentioned to them that I think not having more respect for the land may have been the problem. It appeared that they may have been overfishing, over-mining, and over timbering.

Portlock, Alaska

Unfortunately, I think many people who witness these beings may have allowed their fear to dominate the situation, and if they had a gun, might be tempted to bag one to save the villagers, or perhaps simply hope that a carefully placed bullet would save their life. Over the years I've had a few people tell me they have seen one in their rifle scope, but after a careful look, realized that it had a very humanlike expression on its face, so they didn't shoot. A few people used to criticize our unwillingness to shoot one at the Sierra Camp, just so the species could be identified by science. Trust me, having been in their presence and heard the amplitude of their huge vocalizations, I didn't want to shoot unless one of them tore through the shelter's walls and I became threatened. I'm sure the other guys felt the same. Also, although we had high-powered guns with us, I'm not sure how effective they would have been. Had we used them, we would probably all be completely deaf now, for sure; a couple of .44 Magnums and three .7mm rifles would make a powerful noise, especially all at once and in such tight quarters.

In July of 1924, two miles east of Mount St. Helens in Oregon, Fred Beck claimed to have shot one "dead-on" near his mining camp and said it fell off into a four-hundred-foot gorge, but they never found the body. Over the years I've heard of other reports of hunters having shot one, but again, no remains were found.

Where does research on these beings go if someone does not produce a body? Most people, if they believe in the possibility of the existence of Bigfoot, think that they must be an unidentified great ape that has learned to become "one" with their environment and is an expert at camouflaging. Hunters could be walking past one and not see it.

Years ago, I interviewed a hunter who was patiently waiting for the sunrise to spot a deer. She said the sun was coming up and she began to scope the large meadow from the tree line. The meadow had burned several years earlier, and a few stumps remained. As she stealthily watched, one of those stumps got up and walked away. She claimed it was a Bigfoot. Over the years, I've heard several very similar reports.

So are these beings just a very stealthy great ape in the woods? And if so, what happens to their bodies when they die? That question has been asked innumerable times; if they exist, at some point a body should be found. Anyone who has spent a good bit of time in the backcountry understands how nature works. A few years back, a bear was injured and managed to wander onto my ranch in California. Unfortunately, it died there, and if I got within smelling distance, or the carcass was upwind that day, it became very noticeable. I called the fish and game department, but they didn't want to mess with it. So because it died around a big patch of poison oak and on my property, I left it there. A year later it was hardly noticeable. Two years later nobody would ever have known it had been there. The moral of this story is that nature cleans up after itself.

One year on my way into the Sierra Camp, I came across a fresh, recently deceased, carcass of a deer—actually, very fresh, along with very fresh bear tracks, some with skid marks, suggesting a rapid departure. Because the tracks were big and fresh, and because the tracks went into a close-by thicket, I picked up my pace. I probably disturbed that bear's afternoon snack, and I certainly did not want to contribute to its dinner. A few days later on my way out, most of the deer had been eaten. On my next trip in a few weeks later, all that was left were some bones, and they had been chewed on by varmints. The following year any remaining bones were scattered and hard to find. After that, you would never know anything had happened there. So this should answer those naysayer's questions.

I remember the late Dr. Grover Krantz (1931–2002), an anthropologist at Washington State University, stating that when an animal knows it is going to die, it will pick its spot . . . unless, of course, it doesn't know when it'll get its departure order.

Dr. Krantz was not a proponent of the recordings that we captured. Although we both resided close to each other in Washington state, he did not want to talk with me. As a classical anthropologist, he believed only humans have the vocal ability for speech, so he must have figured the Sierra vocalizations that we captured could not be trustworthy. I'm not sure what he thought about Dr. Kirlin's (a professor of electrical engineering) study establishing the vocalizations on the tapes that he said represented an animal over eight feet tall compared to the human vocal mechanism. And there was no evidence of the tape's speed being altered. The size compared to the human's vocal range was also corroborated by Dr. Benson from Texas A&M University. He said the amplitude represented an animal eight feet, five inches tall. Could it be that Dr. Krantz hadn't read the evidence?

If Bigfoot is just another unidentified great ape they would eventually die, but we might never find any remains unless it was a recent death, and someone reported it. However, you'd think that after so many people report having seen one alongside the road, watching them go by, that eventually one would step out in front of a vehicle and BAM, we would have scientific evidence or at least a wrecked car with hair on it. But what I have heard from reports more times than not is that after passing one alongside the road, people have seen it crossing the road in their rear-view mirror. That would suggest that they have enough intelligence to know to wait.

My personal experiences around these beings at the Sierra Camp suggest to me that they are extremely intelligent. During those early years of the seventies, we underestimated them and their level of intuitiveness. The Sierra Giants are a clever primate with attributes that still confuse many people who encounter them. I'm sure that they are much more than what many want to believe. Humans are supposed to be the most evolved species on this planet, yet with all this technology we still can't seem to find this species, yet they seem to be able to find us. That should cause some to ponder, even though the Mountain Gorilla was not officially recognized until 1904.

Fred Beck, whom I mentioned earlier, claimed to have shot one, but also stated that he was sure the beings were paranormal. Before he shot one, he and the other miners found large humanlike prints in a large, muddy area, but the prints suddenly stopped. It would have had to have jumped 160 feet, he wrote, to reach an area where the ground would not have left a print. Most researchers would say that a helicopter must have picked it up. Really? So they say that reports like that must be hoaxed. Nothing can just disappear. That statement is made by those who have not looked into how many things can work and might want to read chapter 7 on cloaking.

For sure, they are an unidentified ape in the woods, just flesh and blood, they say, but I say nothing is "just" flesh and blood. There is more to humans than "just" flesh and blood, and there's more to Bigfoot than "just" flesh and blood.

"Flesh and blood" will eventually die, but does our consciousness, our energy being, our soul? There are many people who claim that our consciousness is not part of the brain, that indeed it is our soul. When some people flatline on the operating table but are later revived, they are able to recall looking at themselves from above the table and actually describe happenings that they would not have known from laying on that table while sedated.

If Einstein and Hawking are right about the nature of energy, then after our bodies die, our consciousness, being energetic in nature, would change forms. Religious people would call that going to heaven or else to a dark place where one burns. A theoretical physicist would probably say that a person's energy will just change its form.

5

FLESH AND BLOOD

For years I have listened to people make the argument that these beings are flesh and blood only. I disagree with the "only" part of that. Nothing living is flesh and blood "only." Humans are not flesh and blood only. There is more to the *Homo sapiens sapiens* than just flesh and blood. What gives us our consciences, our emotions, or our ability to alter certain things with our thoughts? Some people have homed in on many other attributes that humans seem to have, such as telepathy, telekinesis, clairvoyance, and even remote viewing, which is how some people view an environment from anywhere in the world without physically being there; it can and does happen.

Remote viewing did not spring into existence overnight. Its earliest ancestors can be traced back thousands of years to the days of the early Greeks and beyond. In the late 1960s and early 1970s, out-of-body experiments were conducted in New York City by researchers at the American Society for Psychical Research.

In the mid-seventies government support for the growing program moved from the CIA to the Defense Intelligence Agency (DIA), as well as certain other military organizations. In 1978 the US Army created a unit to use remote viewing operationally in collecting intelligence against foreign adversaries. This program continued under Army sponsorship until 1986, when the operational and research arms of the government remote viewing program were combined under the leadership of DIA. In about 1991, DIA renamed the program "Stargate." It was popularized in the 1990s upon the declassification of certain documents related to the Stargate Project, a twenty-million-dollar research program that had started in 1975 and was sponsored by the US government in an attempt to determine any potential military application of psychic phenomena.

So, do we still think that these attributes are just illusionary or maybe trickery? Classical science is based upon everything being physical and material, measurable and predictable. Is that true? Yes, it is partly true, but I'm afraid I have to disagree with the "everything" part (unless we break that word up: *every thing*, meaning everything material). Since nobody could answer my boyhood question—"How big is the universe?"—something is missing from the physics that I had been taught and, unfortunately, is still being taught today as if classical science is all there is. Years ago, I began to question almost everything I'd been taught.

"Trust the science" is what we are conditioned to do, but I think it's the most antiscientific statement ever. Questioning science and asking questions is how we should do science.

In the early 1900s, a new science had come to academia, which began to answer the questions that classical science could not. It was called quantum mechanics, and in 1918 Max Planck received the Nobel Prize for developing the math that established that everything is not measurable or predictable. Quantum science, which is established by mathematical equations, continued to be studied with Einstein, Bohr, Tesla, and many other physicists. Some say that it is just a theory because it cannot be seen, which is BS in my opinion. If it is shown to exist mathematically, then it must be shown to be mathematically incorrect (i.e., disproven mathematically). We will never see all there is to see with our two eyes. So theoretical physics is accepted. The math of quantum physics has shown that there are at least ten different dimensions—nine plus time (which is the fourth), and the environment in which we live is only three-dimensional: length, width, and depth. So other things exist that are outside our 3D perimeters.

Because we live on a planet in a linear 3D environment, we are obliged to live under those rules, so most of us do. Otherwise, we may be considered a paranormal devotee, a.k.a. a *woo-wooer*.

What is a woo-wooer? It's someone whose ideas are outside of the classical box; someone who doesn't accept everything that he or she has been taught as absolute proof; someone who thinks that there must be something going on that we're not being taught in school. However, the woo, or paranormal, is actually pseudoscience—a collection of beliefs or practices mistakenly regarded as being based on scientific method—but in truth, it's not.

To be clear, quantum science and the paranormal are not to be considered the same. I am not a paranormal guy; I research modern science (quantum science) and attempt to explain how, according to that science, many of the strange stuff that was reported to me by observers works on this planet. This includes the many paranormal reports, but many of those can be explained by understanding the math of quantum science.

Years ago, I asked a professor who is involved in the Bigfoot arena about using quantum physics in our search for the answers to the many mysteries surrounding these giants, and he said that he wouldn't discuss that aspect with me. Hmm . . . I know this man to be a religious man who associates himself with a large church. So he surely believes in God. Where is God if not in another dimension other than our 3D perception? Other dimensions that are outside the three that we all live and work in exist within the rules of quantum physics. He said that he has to wear different hats, depending on the subject. I understand that completely, although I am not in that mindset.

Professors who are in the position to teach others are obligated by the discipline that covers their area of study. Many of those in leadership are the ones who create the narrative for us. Most teachers mean well, but they, too, have been conditioned in classical science, and their job depends on teaching what they were taught and what they are being paid to teach.

Quantum physics aims to uncover the properties and behaviors of the building blocks of nature. While many quantum experiments examine very small objects, such as electrons and photons, quantum phenomena are all around us, beginning at a very small scale and continuing throughout the cosmos.

In my second book, *The Quantum Bigfoot*, the subtitle is, "Bringing Science and spirituality back together," and I quote several scientists. These smart and educated people have a lot to offer. So what worked for Tesla, Einstein, Bohr, and others should be good enough for all of us. According to quantum physics, energy cannot die; it looks like we are all spiritual beings occupying a biological body, which will die, but our soul (consciousness) won't, like it or not. Tesla, Einstein, and other physicists also studied the Vedic Sanskrit, which originated from cuneiform tablets, the oldest known written language. When researching this I realized that all of it originated from the Anunnaki, also known as the "Powerful Ones" from the sky. Some say that they represented giants or the Fallen Ones from the Bible. Is this just religion, or is it history? Because Vedic Sanskrit writes about issues outside of classical 3D thinking, it's considered religious and not used inside mainstream science.

Cuneiform tablet

Could Bigfoot be a remnant of the Anunnaki? As written, the Anunnaki were deities from the cosmos, also known as the Shiny Ones, the Powerful Ones, the Sky People, Giants, etc. Sound familiar? They inhabited Earth and are responsible for much of the technology that kicked humanity into gear. So it makes sense to me that the Nephilim (mentioned in the first chapter of the Bible) may have originally been hybrids from the Anunnaki. However, the Nephilim (hybrids from the Anunnaki) were not good for the earth and thought to have been destroyed during the deluge.

Could some of the Nephilim have gone underground and not been destroyed? Could that be how Bigfoot stays so elusive, by living underground? And perhaps many of these beings are remnants of the Nephilim. But, again, over eons, many have come up and been seen; they may have crossbred with indigenous people and therefore been diluted down, becoming more humanlike.

Many Bigfoots display nonclassical attributes but are certainly in flesh-and-blood bodies and are experiencing life on (or in) this planet with us. Do Bigfoots have some of the same attributes as *Homo sapiens*? Yes, although classical science has not established the species, I believe that these giants are part human with some of the same DNA that we have, and I think I have the data that supports that in this book.

Therefore, "flesh and blood only" is out the window for me and for anyone who wants to understand and is ready to acknowledge the fact that there is so much more out there when their thinking steps out of their conditioning. For example like those who can't explain how that certain feeling came into their mind regarding Aunt So-and-So, and then the phone rings and it was Aunt So-and-So. Or to explain how déjà vu works (that feeling that you have already seen and know what is going to happen next), may I suggest that you reconsider the "only" part of "flesh and blood"?

6

MANIFESTATION CODE AND DIMENSIONS

Are there more than three dimensions that we can reach now? If so, where? We don't see them—why not? Perhaps they are not in the ether of the cosmos; maybe they are actually within us, just waiting to be understood. And what about different frequencies, and how do we discover those?

Could Bigfoot understand other dimensions and other frequencies? I think that everyone should try to understand dimensions, how frequencies work, and that some Bigfoots have sapience and perhaps know how to manipulate frequencies. How could I think that's possible? Because they have very, very expansive vocal abilities—much more than humans. And maybe they use that quality to alter themselves. First, however, let's see what science has to say about dimensions. Paraphrased from phys.org[1]:

Dimensions are simply the different facets of how we perceive reality. We are immediately aware of the three dimensions that surround us daily—Beyond these three visible dimensions, scientists believe that there are many more. The theory assumes that the universe exists in ten different dimensions. These different aspects are what govern the universe, the fundamental forces of nature.

The first dimension, A good description of a one-dimensional object is a straight line, which exists only in terms of length and has no other discernible qualities. Add to it a second dimension, and you get an object that becomes a 2-dimensional shape (like a square).

The third dimension involves depth. The perfect example of this is a cube, which exists in three dimensions and has a length, width, depth, and hence volume. Beyond these three lie the seven dimensions which are not immediately apparent to us, but which can still be perceived

Scientists believe that the fourth dimension is time, which governs the properties of all known matter at any given point. The other dimensions are where the deeper possibilities come into play, and explaining their interaction with the others is where things get tricky.

The fifth and sixth dimensions are where the notion of possible worlds arises. If we could see on through to the fifth dimension, we would see a world slightly different from our own which would give us a means of measuring the similarities between our world and other possible ones.

In the sixth, we would see a plane of possible worlds. In theory, if you could master the fifth and sixth dimensions, you could travel back in time or go to different futures.

In the seventh dimension, you have access to the possible worlds that start with different initial conditions. Whereas in the fifth and sixth, the initial conditions were the same and subsequent actions were different, here, everything is different from the very beginning of time. The eighth dimension again gives us a plane of such possible universe histories, each of which begins with different initial conditions and branches out infinitely.

In the ninth dimension, we can compare all the possible universe histories, starting with all the different possible laws of physics. In the tenth and final dimension, we arrive at the point in which everything possible and imaginable is covered. Beyond this, nothing can be imagined by us in our 3D reality, which makes it the natural limitation of what we can conceive in terms of dimensions.

The existence of these additional six dimensions which we cannot perceive is necessary for String Theory for there to be consistency in nature. The fact that we can perceive only four dimensions of space can be explained by one of two mechanisms: either the extra dimensions are compactified on a very small scale, or else our world may live on a 3-dimensional submanifold corresponding to a brane, on which all known particles besides gravity would be restricted (a.k.a. brane theory).

How are dimensions part of life? Do we reach other dimensions by using a spiritual staircase and jumping from one step to another? Or is it something we go to with our consciousness; perhaps a different perspective, or vibration, of who we are? Dimensions are a state of consciousness; all humans have those attributes from the moment of birth and are here to learn how to become aware of them and evolve to a higher level through understanding. Once that's completed, we move on to a new and better life outside of linear time.

From all my research into dimensions and frequencies, it seems theoretical physicists do not have a common theory of what they may represent, even though many freely express their understanding. However, I have my own that I will freely express (a cumulation of several) but I like Tesla's statement regarding the Manifestation Code the most. It seems to work with my spiritual understanding, too. Plus, Tesla said, "What one man calls God another calls the laws of physics."

"If you only knew the magnificence of 3, 6, and 9, you would have a key to the universe."[2]

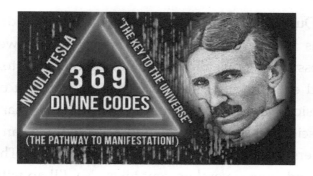

Well, who wouldn't want to know that? We understand and see the three dimensions: length, width, and height. But in that dimension, we move through or experience linear time, moving forward only. In the fourth dimension, there is a theory that time could move backward, too. Time, as we perceive it, only exists in a 3D environment.

A human's embodiment lives and evolves in the third dimension but always will possess two components, a physical body and etheric or energy body (consciousness). The consciousness is the part of a human that cannot die—the energetic or spiritual body, which only changes forms after we pass on from the physical body. We witness a physical mass with our two eyes, but we don't normally see the etheric realm with those eyes; that takes clearing our minds of the rhetoric and conditioning that we deal with daily. It's rare, but some people can see energy forms by entangling with a different frequency. Some people claim to see into the fourth dimension of time and access future and past timelines, and some claim they can see ghostlike images and pixilated beings.

Quantum science tries to understand other dimensions using mathematics. But many suggest we can access those other dimensions using our receptor, the third eye (the pineal gland). This takes us out of the physical and can put us in the etheric plane of consciousness. If effective, and accepted, we can then understand how things can and do work. That is derived from several ancient texts...so, I'll go with the one from Egyptian history, relating to the third eye. Why? Because we all have a pineal gland (third eye). And I also think that Bigfoot has one too.

"The third eye refers to the gate that leads to the inner realms and spaces of higher consciousness. The third eye often symbolizes a state of enlightenment. The third eye is often associated with religious visions, clairvoyance, the ability to observe chakras and auras, precognition, and out-of-body experiences."[3]

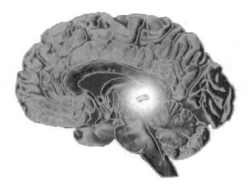

Pineal gland

To be who we were designed to be, and to evolve

the way we are supposed to, we must live in and experience the third dimension. Generally it's just full of challenges and adverse trials to deal with in life. We must learn how to respond to those challenges with our higher self, which is available to all. Once we have become enlightened via the pineal gland, our receptor, we are able to understand the sixth dimension. That's when we realize and appreciate who we are as a human and can manipulate subatomic particles occurring in the nucleus of every atom, for example by performing miracles, healing others, etc. We can reach this while in our three-dimensional environment. We don't disjoin with the third dimension to be enlightened to the sixth, our creative state.

I believe our ultimate objective is to be a light being, someone who experiences the ninth dimension and becomes like our makers (more on light and sound in chapter 10).

So, what does this humanistic idea have to do with Bigfoot? In my opinion, many of these giants were given a DNA upgrade by higher frequential beings long before humans were created. They were not made like us, but their creators knew how to manipulate their DNA so they could alter their frequency from matter to energy, because matter and energy are interchangeable according to Dr. Paul Dirac[4] and Einstein. (See also chapter 7 on cloaking.)

They were not programmed for the ninth dimension like we were, but they are able to cloak in and out of the fourth dimension of time, going out of our perception. Linear time as we perceive it in this third dimension always moves forward, so I've heard. However, my thought is that when our consciousness moves out of this body into the fourth dimension, we can go either way in time, forward or backward.

Once we leave this embodiment, there's more going on, for sure. That's when something really good can happen. Rarely, in just one lifetime, are humans able to take care of all the things we responded to incorrectly during the past lives that we have all had. I think that I know what some religious people are being told and being quoted now. In Hebrews 9:27 it is said: "And it is appointed unto man once to die, but after that the judgment . . ." I don't disagree with that. Someday, our body will die, and then our consciousness (which cannot die) decides how to balance our past lives' negativities, for instance by being born into another family, in another time, or on another planet. We all need to evolve by understanding love and compassion.

This is how I think we evolve to our higher self: we'll embrace the challenges that are ahead by accepting them and being glad they are in front of us allowing us to grow and finally become a member of the collective consciousness of our universe. I think it's all about responding correctly to experiences. Never consider yourself a victim.

In one form or another we have all been alive at

different times for eons (our consciousness, embodied in different forms), but obviously we have more learning to do and more to experience, otherwise we would not be here. We have been put on this planet in our present embodiment so we can evolve during different times, but this dimension is the one that allows each of us the time we need to get better, and better, and better. We do this through our actions, which are enhanced by meditation that raises our vibrational frequency. When we've learned to effectively meditate, we allow information into our consciousness through our third eye. That information will become part of our heart's brain, interpreted as a gut feeling. The heart must become coherent with our outside-thinking brain, the one that's stuck on our shoulders, the one that was conditioned. The analytical brain will often not follow the heart's leadership; sometimes the brain analyses too much. If we turn right, we could have made a lot more money than if we had turned left, but our gut feeling (heart) said to turn left, which would have been correct.

By following those three elements, which can work together through meditation, we will be led into doing the right thing: to evolve and understand who we were originally made to be, that is, ninth-dimensional light beings.

During meditation (something we should all make time for) we can visualize our seven chakras in alignment, all pulsating rhythmically; it takes practice to empty the outside thoughts. Some of us may want the quietness—if that's possible. Either way, we must be still and empty our minds of all the BS that infiltrates our daily lives.

This earth is our testing ground. We are here with the opportunity to experience things. How we respond to those things will determine our frequency, up or down. If what we do intentionally hurts others in any way, then at some time we will need to correct that action, apologizing if possible. Advancing to a higher understanding is done by responding to all issues with a caring, compassionate attitude.

So there: I have finally satisfied my previous wonderment about Nikola Testa's 3-6-9 manifestation statement.

To summarize: Everything, from the cosmos to the subatomic level, is (or was) brought about by a consciousness, which is above anything we could possibly comprehend while in our 3D state. That consciousness is energy, and it creates frequencies that vibrate. In the beginning was the "WORD" and that word frequency created light when it reached the 49th octave. For more about light and sound, see chapter 10.

In the Bible, many different names have been used for God? I believe there was a misleading construct, possibly by the Aramaic culture, when they used the name for God. In the oldest known written language (cuneiform), *God* is a plural noun, and from my research we need to consider the ninth-dimension beings as the ones who created *Homo sapiens sapiens* in their image—in other words: light beings. As it's said in 1 John 1:5–9: "God is Light." And that is, or will be, a hard pill for many to swallow. I suggest that anyone who questions this finding to research and find out who changed *Elohim* in the cuneiform (*God* in Hebrew) from plural to singular, and for what reason. I suspect that it may have worked better with the translation(s). Usually, however, literature is changed for control by the powers in charge.

However, if there are several gods, could some be bad and some be good? Many of the stories in the Old Testament did not seem cohesive. On one hand, there is a god that is life-giving and caring toward humans, and on the other hand, there is one who is cruel.[5]

In 325 AD, the Roman emperor Constantine called a council in the city of Nicaea. The council brought together bishops from all over Christendom to resolve several divisive issues and ensure unity of the church because too many factions were spreading different ideas. The emperor wanted one religion for his people to follow. From that council, the four Gospels of Matthew, Mark, Luke, and John are the only ones that were accepted. All the other books were not accepted at that time, including the Book of Enoch, which did not fit their narrative and was never canonized. Enoch writes about the heavens, the Fallen Ones, and many other interesting issues that fell outside of the council's 3D paradigms.

Ninth-dimensional entities have been around for

eons (billions of years). They are considered light beings and do not have, or need, an embodiment. However, they are so advanced that they are able to embody anything and become matter. Basically, there are no limits on what they can do. They created the human species from the troglodytes. Much earlier, though, some Bigfoots were also created from troglodytes but not given the same attributes that humans got, like the DNA to become light beings. Later, those ninth-dimensional entities limited our lifespan by altering our telomeres.

In my opinion, light beings were the Anunnaki (also known as the Powerful Ones from the sky) and sponsored the cuneiform text, which was the first-known written language to be used by several cultures in ancient Mesopotamia, mainly the Sumerians. However, that written text trickled to the Babylonians, Akkadians, Persians, and Aramaic cultures. The cuneiform text was used to write at least a dozen different languages and is the root of the modern Christian Bible. Over many centuries and cultures, written languages were altered to fit the current idealistic nature of leadership.

Many of the Anunnaki, who I believe to be the Fallen Ones from the biblical text, crossbred with different cultures, creating demigods. They were on this planet prior to the deluge as well as after. Many other beings from different frequencies have visited Earth and have also manipulated different species. (See chapter 9, Hybridization.)

Some of those other advanced entities exist in the fifth dimension. Many are on earth now and are cloaked until they lower their density into the third dimension. When that happens, we can see them. We see matter in this frequency, unless of course you can see energy.

Third Dimension = All humans have multiple embodiments for learning.

Sixth Dimension = Our consciousness has learned, and we are able to create.

Ninth Dimension = We are what we were originally designed to be: Children of the Light, created by the light beings, the Powerful Ones (Elohim). We are special (Ephesians 5:8).

1. We are complete with love and compassion for all of creation
2. We will reign as Kings and Priests in eternity (Isaiah 61:6).
3. We will live forever without the need of a body but can embody any living entity in the universe.

We will not achieve the ninth dimension of consciousness without first learning love and compassion in the third dimension, then you know and understand the sixth (the creative state) and know that those made in the image of the creator of all things can go to the ninth. All is good as long as artificial intelligence (see chapter 14) doesn't alter humans too much. We must stay completely human. (And by that I don't mean that we couldn't get a heart transplant or have a knee replaced.)

I believe the tenth dimension is the ultimate consciousness by which everything began.

7

CLOAKING: QUANTUM PHYSICS AT WORK

We hear it often: "That thing disappeared right in front of my eyes." Could that happen? And if so, how?

In my last book, *The Quantum Bigfoot*, I wrote a chapter on invisibility. In that chapter, I gave a lot of history relating to invisibility, but since then I've collected the scientific rule that I think could govern that ability. Of course, the science is quantum physics, but I think it all fits with what so many credible people are reporting these days. And when people who are not in collaboration with others all report the same thing, well, there must be something to it. I hope to build on that idea in this chapter.

In 1933, Professor Paul Dirac won the Nobel Prize for his equation that mathematically established that matter changes into energy, or, in other words, antimatter. This was later confirmed by CERN (The European Organization for Nuclear Research) in 2012 with the Hadron Collider. So it's a fact that matter, which at the most minute level of all physical existence, Bigfoot included (through frequency), can turn into energy. There's this idea that energy cannot die; it can only change forms. We do not see it happen with our two eyes, but it happens. As Albert Einstein said, "Energy and matter are interchangeable, find the frequency of anything and its matter can change... and that's all there is to it. What we have called matter is energy, whose vibration has been so lowered as to be perceptible to the senses."[1]

Paul Dirac 1902 – 1984

So, YES, absolutely, those who have reported that they saw one disappear are not necessarily being ridiculous, delusional, untruthful, or crazy after all. Much too often we researchers want to refer those people to the funny farm. If we can't see it with our two eyes, it just does not exist...but this attitude is wrong. Many people do not want to be confused with the facts. However, the science behind how that could happen exists.

Think about it and try not to raise your paradigm umbrella. If Bigfoot can change their matter into energy, perhaps through the manipulation of vibrational frequency, their density would also change, and their trackway would stop. Wouldn't that answer a lot of questions? I guess a helicopter didn't pick them up after all.

Everything is energy, frequency, and vibration – Nikola Tesla

The idea that aliens had traveled through the cosmos to get to this planet has been frequently criticized by those who believe it would have taken them thousands of years. Of course, that thinking is using Einstein's idea that "Nothing can travel faster than the speed of light." Nothing means *no thing*. What about our consciousness? It certainly goes faster than light, for instance from one thought to another. That is quantum entanglement, and it's real; we all experience it daily. So could aliens travel using a method other than the speed of light, such as consciousness? That idea would also give us an understanding of dimensions, because when a UAP goes out of our 3D limitations, it would longer be seen.

It's happening now almost daily. I believe that

many aliens communicate and travel using consciousness—a big step above the way most of us think today. Plus, if Bigfoot is part alien, they may have learned how to communicate the same way, i.e., mindspeak. Another traveling thought, though theoretical, is that aliens use wormholes.

Wormhole

If you believe as I do that over long periods of time, different types of aliens have been on this planet, then you may also choose to believe that they've messed with the genome of different species (altering their DNA). Therefore, there could well be different types of these giant beings on this planet. They are not all the same; some may cloak, and some may not be able to do that. Some of them may have been given the gene for language, and some may not. Over eons, I believe that many have been diluted through crossbreeding with indigenous people. This would make many of them more humanlike.

Due to perhaps crossbreeding with human people many of these giants could be different. Many have probably been on this planet for eons and just evolved through the ranks as relic hominids. They possibly have very few unusual attributes but have adapted to their environment and have learned to camouflage well.

Comparing prints

For many years I was challenged with the type of

prints that we witnessed and cast at the Sierra Camp after hearing vocal outbursts the prior evening. The prints are different from the accepted Roger Patterson prints from Bluff Creek, California in 1967. However, year after year the prints that we witnessed were all of the same configuration in various sizes: very splayed with very little arch.

Everything is supposed to evolve. Perhaps we were dealing with a different species of giants. Why didn't we see them more often? Through the cracks in the shelter's walls, we could clearly hear them, and very often they were very close. Any glimpses that we got were fleeting. At that time, none of us were familiar with how all things actually work throughout the universe, and we never considered that they may be cloaking. We had all been conditioned to only believe in what we could see, feel, or touch.

I suggest those who want to know more about how all things work, from the atom to the stars, catch up on modern science, quantum physics in particular. It's not pseudoscience or the "woo," but it might just give answers to some lingering questions you've had with a "strangeness" that you experienced while in the backwoods.[2]

When in that dark, spooky, woodsy forest, something to consider is the human eyes' frequency range. As with everything, light has a frequency, which sits between 430 THz and 770 THz. So there's more going on than what meets our two eyes. Everywhere we go, there are spirits in other realities moving in, around, and sometimes through us. They are invisible to us as they are in another frequency of existence, one that we are not tuned into. It is like a TV: you watch one channel, but to see another program, you will need to change the channel. Some TV sets are built so you can see more than one image at a time, just as some people are able to see spirits and other realms whereas the average person is only set to one channel at a time.

Something else to consider, if you are in the forest, is that a bear's olfactory sense is way better than ours —twenty times better. So although a bear does not see well, if he gets a whiff of you, he either rapidly goes by, leaving a dusty cloud, or he's circling around behind you—something to think about. If it's a sow with cubs, you'd better stand still or at least get ready for an experience you may not want. So if you're stalking a bear, stay downwind. Should you decide to take your dog, its olfactory sense is less than a bear's but still seven times better than ours.

Understanding our human limits is important to our survival. Humans do not hear ultrasound or infrasound like many animals do. Our normal hearing is between about 20Hz to 20,000Hz. A dog can normally hear above that range, and large animals, like elephants, giraffes, tigers, and maybe Bigfoot, often communicate in the lower infrasound range; this sound can affect humans, but we can only hear, see, and smell within the limitations of our human construct.

So if you are a woodsy-type person or planning a

trip to Africa, I suggest that these restrictive humanoid factors be considered. Humans are limited by our senses, but often when our brain cannot assimilate something it will usually fill in the holes with what it has been taught. Researchers of the paranormal are having a field day as people are reporting experiences with what they term ghosts, angels, extraterrestrials, interdimensional beings, and even Bigfoot. I would hope that those experiences would lead them to an understanding of not just our human limitations, but also that of modern science. As Dr. Edgar Mitchell said, "There are no unnatural or supernatural phenomenon, only very large gaps in our knowledge of what is natural . . . we should strive to fill those gaps of ignorance. [. . .] It takes classical and quantum sciences together for clear perception." These two statements by Dr. Mitchell hit home with me; we need to keep learning.

An anomaly that often separates many researchers is the subject of portals; however, many have obviously not investigated them. Many are often witness to the phenomenon but don't understand how magnetic fields work. Magnetic fields exist in many places on this planet, and everything living has a magnetic field; these are known as auras. As reported by David J. Brown:

> NASA recently reported that a University of Iowa plasma physicist Jack Scudder discovered that there are regions in the Earth's magnetic field that directly

connect it to the magnetic field of the sun, across 93 million miles of space.

These mysterious regions, known as "magnetic portals" are thought to be opening and closing dozens of times every day.[3]

Because portals are not generally seen with our two eyes, it's difficult for many people to accept that they exist, but they do. Jack Scudder continues, "We call them X-points or electron diffusion regions, they're places where the magnetic field of Earth connects to the magnetic field of the Sun, creating an uninterrupted path leading from our own planet to the sun's atmosphere 93 million miles away."[4]

If some of these beings can disappear, it may have something to do with portals. It's been reported that the Skinwalker Ranch in Utah, has a portal and Bigfoot has been seen coming through that magnetic energy field (which would be a portal).

Okay, so now there are at least three choices to consider when "Now you see it, now you don't" is a situation that presents itself in our reality:

1. They pass through a portal.
2. They change their density from matter to energy and therefore their mass goes out of our perception, they become weightless, and their trackway stops.
3. They are a relic hominid only, experts at camouflage, so they don't disappear. All

those people who claim that they saw one disappear were not credible and their eyewitness reports are not to be considered.

There's matter and antimatter, but to some, it doesn't matter.

8

INTERVENTION AND KARMA

I s anyone or anything supposed to interfere with the decisions we all have to make in everyday life? Does Bigfoot intervene? Over the years I have listened to people who claim that Bigfoot mind-speaks to them and told them what to do. On the other side, I have listened to nonbelievers say that what happened must have been God's will, or "the devil made me do it." Could it be that many of us try to put blame elsewhere and be a victim rather than putting the blame where it really belongs? Nobody should ever consider themself a product of their environment, but it can happen if we allow it.

The following questions present themselves: Why are some folks lucky in life, have it all, and are born with that "silver spoon" in their mouths? Yet some go through every day trying to eke out enough to feed their family? Why are some born mentally or physically challenged? Or we see a young, healthy, twenty-two-year-old man come home from a war with limbs missing, or, far too many times, not come home at all? Surely the ones born with handicaps were not guilty of much wrongdoing, if any, and the twenty-two-year-old war hero hasn't had time to screw things up too badly. Could that thinking be wrong? How could any of this be from a fair and loving god, and how do all these issues balance? Are they supposed to balance? What about karma? How do humans evolve into something better? More education doesn't make a person wiser, just smarter . . . maybe.

For years I have been asked: If aliens and Bigfoot are on this earth, why don't they help us? This earth and we humans are in trouble. If they are so advanced and humanlike, why don't they come out and join civilization? After all, aliens would surely be more advanced than us.

These are good questions, and I say just wait, it's coming. But first, this earth and the humans on it are supposed to evolve into to a positive life from their own decisions. I think the experiences we all have are supposed to happen. Why? It's our choice to react to them . . . and how we react is very important to raising, or unintentionally lowering, our personal frequency. I think Bigfoot is part human and, like us, has a vibrational frequency which, again like us, can be altered at will.

"If you want to find the secrets of the universe, think in terms of energy, frequency and vibration."[1] Nikola Tesla.

Everything, at its most minuscule level, is energy, vibrating at a frequency. You, me, and Bigfoot—so let's go from there.

As mentioned earlier, science says that after our body dies our energy changes forms, so do we get multiple chances to correct our bad decisions? What happens if that doesn't happen prior to leaving the embodiment we're now occupying? Could it be that we get to come back and try again? Although I was conditioned one way while growing up around churched people, I've come to think differently now.

Many religions believe that we do come back and have chances to correct our bad decisions. That actually makes sense to me, especially when you see a five-year-old kid flawlessly playing Beethoven or another singing opera without going flat . . . ever. Or better yet, when a child seems to know another language without having been taught that language, how does that work?

There are many people who conduct past-life regression sessions by hypnotizing their patient and helping them to remember issues they've had in a previous life. Could this be so we have a better chance to change our previous rude and improper decisions?

Many say that Bigfoot-type beings are here to help us. If so, how do we receive that information if they are not supposed to interfere with our karma? Many say that Bigfoot can mindspeak to them. I've never had that happen to me—that I know of, anyway. I always try to consider what I was thinking about that may have been responsible for a specific thought coming into my head. The giant beings that I interacted with were saying something to me in an audible voice. For years I have wondered what they were trying to relate to me that I didn't understand. My guess now is that I was too analytical and wasn't open enough to catch what they were saying because of my brain processor. Since that time, I have learned (and am still learning) how to meditate and how to receive from the universal consciousness.

My brain is getting less analytical and is becoming more coherent with my heart (e.g., gut feelings). How do we line up our heart, brain, and pineal gland (third eye) to become one with the other? I believe it is critical—if we want to learn how—to raise our personal vibrational frequency to get us to where we are supposed to be. That's how we get better, for instance when we learn to "turn the other cheek," or not get angry at minor things. Like getting irritated at an elderly lady, in what seems to be a stalled car, who accidentally doubled her medication and didn't go when the light turned green. We make ourselves better when we respond with compassion and love. So, again, could the forest beings want to help us? Perhaps they shouldn't interfere with what we are supposed to react to, or with our karma. To this day I still do not know what those giants were trying to say to me.

But they did interfere with us at the Sierra Camp. Why? We all have choices, as does Bigfoot. So I figure that whatever they wanted to communicate to me, it must have been important enough for them to interfere. It has certainly compelled me to speak about the enigmatic experiences and the unanswered mysteries that the camp still holds—and also to write this book. In my senior years, I decided not to hold back on talking about those events, so I talk freely at conferences, on podcasts, while filming, and in my books. Some of the people who think I have a story to tell used to draw the line at the woo and don't want to be considered a nominee for the funny farm, so they don't ask those woo-woo questions. Nothing can be paranormal . . . right? I think, however, that many people are experiencing unusual events when around these giants, and those events are not answered by classical science. Newtonian physics seemingly does not satisfy them, so they have begun to consider quantum theory. Quantum physics answers many of the so-called paranormal questions, but they are not the same; after all, Nikola Tesla, Albert Einstein, Niels Bohr, and other theatrical physicists of modern science were not paranormal investigators.

Those guys from around a hundred years ago thought outside the box. They knew, as Max Planck knew, that Newtonian science, as important as it is to all of us, cannot answer the deeper questions that we all experience in life. The other guys and I at the Sierra Camp certainly experienced strange stuff that was outside the classical box, and it's taken me years to come forth with a partial understanding.

There is a higher power of consciousness that exists outside our 3D perception of reality, but believe it or not, we are all part of it. It gives us choices that will allow us to raise ourselves to a better level, both in this life and in the afterlife, whatever that may be. We've got to get it right; we can, and we must, do it by making good choices. Nobody, or nothing, can do it for us.

However, if we learn to tune in to the third eye (pineal gland) via meditation, we could be on a much better path for the connection into the universal consciousness, the oneness that so many masters taught.

So, can Bigfoot mindspeak? Perhaps some of them can tune in to our frequency and communicate. We just need to discern if it is our brain working overtime, or if something or someone is trying to get a point across. When a thought comes to me, I stop and consider: Was I thinking about something that brought that thought to me, or was something being suggested to me from another source, perhaps a higher source? Could Bigfoot be connected to that higher source better than most of us, a source that we are capable of reaching?

9

HYBRIDIZATION

Bigfoot and Humans Have a Common Component

The dictionary says that a hybrid is the offspring of two plants or animals of different species or varieties, such as a mule (a hybrid of a donkey and a mare horse). However, supposedly most hybrids are not able to reproduce. There have been five documented accounts of this happening between a mare horse and a jack donkey in the last two hundred years. One jackass out of thousands might be able to reproduce, which would be due to an odd number of chromosomes.[1]

Although I believe the accepted theory of evolution is partly correct, it is obviously incomplete. It does not include the primate who we call Bigfoot and possibly others yet to be discovered.

However, another theory has emerged from a genetic study by Dr. Melba Ketchum, who claimed there was human DNA within several purported samples of Bigfoot; she analyzed these samples and wrote a paper regarding that DNA study. However, most of the academic world gave her a thumbs down, stating that the study must have been contaminated because of a human component found within some of the samples. But now another academic, Kevin Leroy Harter, has come forward with a new study, stating Dr. Ketchum's results may not have been contaminated, but misinterpreted. He called his interpretation "Mito-chondrial Introgression." Perhaps the samples given to Ketchum's lab did not get contaminated but instead there may actually have been natural human DNA in those samples.

Harter's essay[2] suggests introgression and estab-lishment of the human mitochondrial genome within the Sasquatch population, which could result from rare hybrid events involving a human female (the source of the mtDNA) and a male Sasquatch that produce female offspring, which survive to reproduc-tive maturity and backcross within the Sasquatch population. The human mtDNA persists matriarchally, while the nuclear (nuDNA) genome is successively diluted with each backcross, back to the Sasquatch condition (possibly with some lingering isolated human genes). So the phenotype, the physical appear-ance of the population is Sasquatch, although the mtDNA of some or all may be human. But my question is: How did the human DNA actually get in us to start with, and also Bigfoot's DNA?

The reason that humans have only twenty-three pair of chromosomes, yet other primates possess twenty-four, is because (according to classical science) at some point in the human timeline a pair of chromosomes were fused together. That theory has been challenged by a top geneticist, Dr. Francis Collins, a molecular geneticist who was head of the National Institutes of Health in the United States for twelve years. He states "The fusion that occurred as we evolved from the apes has left its DNA imprint here. It is very difficult to understand this observation without postulating a common ancestor."[3]

Out of the ocean and on to the land, throughout the ages, the caveman evolved—yes, before our sapient ancestor, Adam, for all those religious, Bible-totin' folks. Many years ago, I wrote an article explaining my thoughts about the first and second chapter of Genesis and how I thought it seems to be referencing two different types of people. There was the first man who God created and was not denied anything (Genesis 1:29). However, in the second chapter, God had no man to till the soil (Genesis 2:5) and that man was restricted from certain things. So, I suggest that the caveman was here for that first chapter, but in the second chapter God altered the DNA of a primate again and gave him expanded attributes, making him a living soul (Genesis 2:5) but with limitations. That's who we are. But while holding that thought, please consider that I believe that God (Elohim) is plural; explained later in chapter 6.

Therefore, we are hybrids—a cross between the caveman and God. We have special abilities and are connected with these higher-power beings with the input of sapience in our genetics, which I don't think the caveman had. (Note again the plural that I've put in God). However, the giants that we dealt with in the Sierras have sapience.

Could a Bigfootlike being have been here before *Homo sapiens* (us)? Could that being have evolved more and been made for a different reason, but was given a DNA upgrade—not exactly like us, but like us in a way? Going a bit further, could a different high-frequential entity have created another hybrid (us) and made him above the caveman? Could that be who we are?

I am suggesting an alien presence here on this planet. If the cosmos is as large as it appears to be, then there is no end to it, and other life forms could be limitless. I believe that over eons several different types of aliens have visited this earth and experimented with different species here. There's evidence all over the world of highly advanced humanlike beings having been here, and I've personally witnessed some of their remains.

These elongated skulls in Peru had a single parietal (no sagittal suture); many had two small holes in the back of their skull, very large eye sockets, and an unusual mandible.

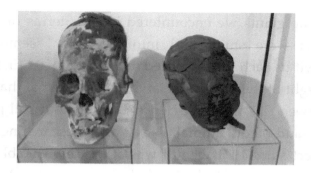

Conforming to academia's classical ways, German archaeologist Klaus Schmidt, who first excavated the site, described Göbekli Tepe as "a sanctuary used by groups of nomadic hunter-gatherers from a wide area, with few or no permanent inhabitants."[4]

Really? Hunter-gatherers did this? That statement suggest that the caveman did it. I don't think so. How advanced would a culture need to be to put these structures together? Whoever they were they must have lived alongside hunter-gatherers.

The giants we encountered in the Sierras of California were smart and intuitive. They seemed to outwit us each time we tried to trick them. At first, we thought of them as just a large apelike animal that has not been classified by science; unusual, but still just a flesh-and-blood animal. Now, after researching this subject since 1971 when I was at the unbreakable age of twenty-nine, I think of them differently. I have accepted that not all things we are taught are the truth. We have been, and still are, being conditioned.

Our government has now told us that the Roswell crash was not really a weather balloon after all, but it was a UFO (now termed UAP) and aliens were on it, I guess it can now be openly discussed now without ridicule.

I have traveled to South America a couple of times, where I found that UAP sightings are commonplace. I traveled there two different times, with two different scientists, to examine the elongated skulls of Peru. For years I've heard reports of Bigfoot having a sagittal crest. I wanted to see if there was a crumb-trail that leads to the north. What I discovered were stories that the Incas warred with the Aztecs and the Mayans in Central America, and they warred with giants in the north. This information took me to the Lovelock Caves where the Native American Paiutes have a story of warring with cannibalistic red-haired giants in what is now called Lovelock, Nevada. This is written about in Sarah Winnemucca's book, *Life Among the Paiutes*.

However, the elongated skulls of Paracas, Peru,

were not totally human. They were hybrids. Brian Foerster, who I was with both times, fostered the DNA study and made the following statement.

"The DNA results actually were incredibly complicated…What it (DNA) does show for sure is that the Paracas elongated skull people were not 100% Native American. Their blood types are very complicated as well, they should be blood type "O" if they are 100% Native American and that's not the case. We are likely looking at a sub-species of humanity as regards to the Paracas… Seems to be a lot of DNA evidence from extreme eastern Europe and extreme western Asia…"[5]

Author, Brian Forester, Richard (photographer), L. A. Marzulli

After reviewing the history of the Paiutes in Nevada and other huge remains that have been discovered in the Sierra mountains, like the Minaret Skull discovered by Dr. Denton, or the Martindale Mummies found in Yosemite, it is clear to me that our experiences at the Sierra Camp add to the knowledge that there is a history of giants in North America, and they are still there. But are they hybrids? The many reports of people who've witnessed these beings up close said that they had a very human look to their faces—a very intelligent look; however, not all of them have a sagittal crest.

April Holloway reported in 2013: "A new study presented to the Royal Society meeting on ancient DNA in London . . . has revealed a dramatic finding: the genome of one of our ancient ancestors, the Denisovans, contains a segment of DNA that seems to have come from another species that is currently unknown to science. The discovery suggests that there was rampant interbreeding between ancient human species in Europe and Asia more than 30,000 years ago. But, far more significant was the finding that they also mated with a mystery species from Asia—one that is neither human nor Neanderthal."[6]

Archologists are discovering more every day about different species who they think may have been cross-breeding with Homo sapiens. But did we have giants in South America who may have had a human component? Could they have moved those 100-ton+ boulders and put them together without mortar? Or was there an understandable science behind that?

Robots might not be limited to science fiction anymore.

Miniature machines can switch from solid to liquid and back again to squeeze into tight spaces and perform tasks like soldering a circuit board, researchers report, January 25 in *Matter*.

This phase-shifting property, is controlled remotely with a magnetic field, is thanks to the metal gallium. Researchers embedded the metal with magnetic particles to direct the metal's movements with magnets. This new material could help scientists develop soft, flexible robots that can shimmy through narrow passages and be guided externally. [...]

Gallium, a metal that melts at about 30° Celsius — just above room temperature. Rather than connecting a heater to a chunk of the metal to change its state, the researchers expose it to a rapidly changing magnetic field to liquefy it. The alternating magnetic field generates electricity within the gallium, causing it to heat up and melt. It will then resolidify when left to cool to room temperature.

Since magnetic particles are sprinkled throughout the gallium, a permanent magnet can drag it around. The magnet can move the material at a speed of about 1.5 meters per second. The upgraded gallium can also carry about 10,000 times its weight. [. . .]

One machine removed a small ball from a model human stomach by melting slightly to wrap itself around the foreign object before exiting the organ. But gallium on its own would turn to goo inside a real human body, since the metal is a liquid at body temperature, about 37° C. A few more metals, such as bismuth and tin, would be added to the gallium in biomedical applications to raise the material's melting point, the authors say. In another demonstration, the material liquefied and rehardened to solder a circuit board.[7]

For years I've thought that the boulders in Peru were either moved with sound frequency or that strong giants moved them, but I couldn't understand how they would have been put together like a puzzle with no mortar. Our science could be catching up.

Over eons, I believe that many types of aliens with higher technology have been on this planet and messed with the DNA of different species, creating different types of hybrids, with different agenda. Perhaps aliens experimented in order to get some type of being for their benefit. This causes me to think that many Bigfoots are good, and some may not be good; it depends on who or what created them and the creators' agenda. The Sierra Giants who we dealt with have language, and they didn't eat us or carry us away, so good for us.

If we put all this together, the conclusion is that the giants who we encountered have a human common denominator and that's language.

Why isn't this the smoking gun that establishes a different kind of hominid who exist on this planet besides the ones in Darwin's theory? It takes a hyoid bone connected to the tongue by many muscles and combined with the nerves to the brain so we can use words to speak what we are seeing or thinking. Just like humans, the Sierra Giants have this, but did all these beings come into existence the same way? If we throw the alien component into the mix and believe that different types of aliens have manipulated the genome of different species, and we then include the variations in the various Bigfoots' foot impressions, their ability for speech (or not), and other unrelated characteristics, they can be different. But the ones in our camp have sapient language.

Here's where I plug in the dilution factor. Native lore, which claims that their women were taken, assumingly for breeding, could cause many of these reported differences. I believe that because of reported crossbreeding with indigenous people, some would be more humanlike than others.

So, do we choose to think that these giant beings could be a hybrid, perhaps a cross between the troglodyte (caveman) and a celestial entity (Anunnaki)? Or are they the biblical Nephilim (i.e., the Fallen Ones), who went underground, stayed on earth, and influenced the Sumerians?

These mysterious giants and their attributes remain an enigma. However, we now have a bit more to think about and chew on . . . like a tough steak. For some it may be a bit hard to swallow . . . especially if you've been conditioned that science must be right, earth is only six thousand years old, and Elvis is still alive. And face it, we've all been conditioned from birth to believe what we've been taught.

10

LIGHT AND SOUND

Besides our recorded vocalizations from these giants, other unusual sounds occurred at the Sierra Camp—sounds that were out of place, metallic/electrical, stampeding horses, door slamming, clicking, etc. Unusual lights came in and out of our camp area, too. In 2016, Keri and I, along with a good friend whom I trusted, road on horseback into the Sierra Camp. Because the shelter had been dismantled the prior year, Keri and I set up a small tent with a screened top. Our friend slept in a hammock about fifty feet away. Early that night we were sitting up in the tent when we witnessed a brightly glowing tub-like light slowly maneuver about four to five feet off the ground from the back of the shelter and watched it until it went out of sight about 150 yards away. There was no sound, and it's not plausible that it was someone with a flashlight; it would be ludicrous for anyone to try and find that camp after dark, even if they knew the way, and especially messing around with men who carried guns. Around midnight, our friend in the hammock witnessed a light coming toward camp from a rocky cliff area and thought it must be someone coming to camp carrying a flashlight. He watched as it worked its way toward us. The next morning, he scoured that area looking for any sign, but did not find anything. There is no trail whatsoever in or around those steep boulders.

Many unusual things have happened at the Sierra Camp that are unexplained. I have learned to expect the unexpected. Different types of sounds and lights can be common. According to an article by Brooke Borel, "researchers at the Lawrence Livermore National Laboratory in California successfully converted sound waves to light radiation by reversing a process that transforms electricity to sound, which is commonly used in cell phones. This is the first time that sound has been converted to light."[1]

And according to an article on the Difference Between website: "light triggers the sensation of seeing and sound stimulates the hearing. Light falls into the category of electromagnetic waves, while sound is a mechanical wave. Light is the most familiar form of electromagnetic waves."[2]

But it all starts with sound waves. Sound is a wave that at its 49th octave will change into visible light. As does everything, light has a frequency too.[3] Light's frequency is between 430 THz and 770 THz, and that's all we can see with our two eyes. Yup, those two eyes require light to see, but there's a lot more around us that those two eyes don't see; it takes the third eye to access and understand many of the things that are really going on. All we need to do is pay attention to it, and although it has the traits of an eye, it does not require light. The ancient Egyptians called it the Eye of Horus, and it's also known as our sixth sense, our connection to the spiritual realm, etc. However, science calls it the pineal gland, but they don't comment on anything unusual or what ancient texts tell us what it's capable of doing for us other than say it's our body clock releasing melatonin so we can know when to sleep. What else could the pineal gland do, and how does it relate to our consciousness?

According to Einstein nothing can go faster than the speed of light (186,300 miles per second). I believe that he was referencing matter, meaning anything physical (nothing . . . *no thing*). It's now been determined through quantum physics that our consciousness and our thoughts are not governed or limited by that speed. Our thoughts are immediate and don't actually travel at all; from your brain to your subject matter is immediate. So how does this relate to light?

Because I was raised in religious circles, I will begin with a little of what the good book has to say about "light." There are scriptures throughout the Bible that reference light and how important it is to us. Not so we can just see with our two eyes, but actually "see" with our third eye. That gets into the pineal gland, which I mentioned at length in my previous book, *The Quantum Bigfoot*, and touched on earlier in this book. However, I'll offer the churchgoer more to ponder, such as why I think spirituality (our consciousness) and quantum physics are synonymous. In Genesis 1:3, God said, "let there be light" (note that sound, the word, was before light). And Matthew (5:14) says "Ye are the light of the world." John (1:4) wrote "In Him [Jesus] was life; and the life was the light of men." By the way, Jesus was the physical man and Christ was the ethereal body—as ONE, just like we were made. Now here's the kicker: 1 John 1:5 says "God is light and in Him there is no darkness." Plus, according to the oldest written language, the cuneiform text (from which many other written languages grew), light beings created humans (see chapter 6).

Years ago, I visited the Oregon Caves just out of Cave Junction in southern Oregon. During the tour, the guide asked us to turn out any light that we might be using. Everybody did. At that point he struck a match. That one little light lit up the whole cave, and the cave was huge. When everything is dark, it doesn't take much.

So God is light (1 John 1:5), and throughout history, beginning specifically with the Anunnaki, it's written that light beings (gods, e.g., the Anunnaki) came from the sky.

As I pointed out in a previous chapter, the word *God* (from the Sumerian cuneiform tablets) is *Elohim* in the Hebrew Bible. That translates to the Powerful Ones (plural) from the ancient Sumerian, Babylonian, and Assyrian texts. These cuneiform tablets are known as the oldest form of written language, estimated to have been written in 3400 BCE and translated into Hebrew between 1000 BCE to about 700 BCE.

Many stories gleaned from our modern Bible seem to align with those Sumerian tablets. The biblical characters of Abraham (father of the Hebrew nation) and his wife Sarah, both who lived in a Sumerian culture, probably would have brought with them information they'd gleaned from those writings. The word *God* does not appear in any of those tablets—not anywhere. There are several words in the Hebrew text that reference God as a singular entity. However, *Elohim*—the Powerful Ones from the cuneiform—is mentioned over 2500 times. Jehovah, Yahweh, El Shaddai, and El Qanna are also used, and all are plural.

The serpent mentioned in the Bible was called the Shiny One. (In Hebrew, *nachash*). The Shiny Ones were known by many names, mentioned in the Book of Enoch and also included in the Ethiopian Bible; these texts were not considered canon in the popularized Bible; however, it is accepted by most scholars and included in the Ethiopian text, which was translated into English in 1821.

In my opinion these beings from the sky are high-vibrational entities and are the ones who created humans. "Let us make man in our image" (Genesis 2:7). In church I was taught that this meant, body, soul, and spirit—the three in one. That interpretation could very well be true, but perhaps it's not all there is to think about. Considering all the different stories referencing God as the responsible entity for many issues, good and sometimes seemingly not good, I think we must realize that the powers in charge (Romans/Jews) felt it necessary to translate Elohim as singular.

These high-vibrational beings are transdimensional, with authority over lower-vibrational entities who also exist in this vast cosmos, but with authority to give us dominion on this planet, and nothing should physically interfere with our choices . . . our evolution. We are special, and no entity anywhere is supposed to interfere with anybody's decisions. Even aliens have free will. However, I believe that all humans rank above them. To be clear, humans were created to be, and have the potential of being, above other aliens of higher frequencies. This is supported in 1 Peter 2:9 it says, "But you are a chosen race, a royal priesthood, a holy nation, a people for his own possession, that you may proclaim the excellencies of him who called you out of darkness into his marvelous light."

Also, I'm on the same page with Tesla, who said "What one man calls God, another calls the laws of physics." And actually, that quote should give a degree of comfort to those who stopped participating in a religion because it was not making sense, and it also might suggest to some, as it did to me, to couple spirituality with modern science (i.e., quantum physics).

How does Bigfoot fit into all this? As stated earlier, I believe that many of them were created by aliens who messed around with the DNA of primates. Although Bigfoot and humans are not the same, these aliens also gave some of these giants a component that we also have: language. I also believe that some of the troglodytes were manipulated prior to humanity being created; they were not made exactly the same as us, perhaps the result of aliens experimenting with different species or having a hybridization program (discussed in chapter 11). They were not given the benefits that we'd been given by the Powerful Ones, such as dominion, being in their image, or having the ability to regain the high-frequential status we were originally made for.

So, do these giants (i.e., Bigfoot) have anything over humans besides being so big, strong, and elusive? If everything is energy, I must say that some also have the benefit of being able to change their vibrational frequency, which can mean that they have been given the ability to go out of our perception (by creating the right vibrational frequency) and go through the time (fourth) dimension, going out of our perception by cloaking (see also chapter 7).

Over the years I've heard many stories of light anomalies being associated with Bigfoot sightings, and at different times I witnessed unusual lights at the Sierra Camp. Is this important in our understanding of

Bigfoot? I believe that these lights are a form of energy and have intelligence. A few years ago, David Paulides and his videographer joined me in the Sierra Camp for a short documentary. In that DVD (*Missing 411, The Hunted*), he reproduced an elongated light that Keri and I witnessed two years earlier as it slowly passed by our open-top tent—it was definitely controlled, not random, and navigated its way through the trees. We didn't know what to think, but nothing that happens at that camp would surprise me.

As mentioned, a musical note turns into light at the 49th octave. The process of turning sound into light is called *sonoluminescence*. Chakras are often referred to in yoga practice, used to describe the way energy moves in the body. The word *chakra* is the Sanskrit word for *wheel* because they are said to be spinning forces of energy in the body.

When I meditate, I get comfortable, bring my mind to a neutral state, and often I will listen to the different sound frequencies that are associated with the chakras. The history of the chakra system goes back to the Indus valley civilization, as far back as around 1500 BC. So to those who have been taught that yoga is an evil religion, I suggest delving into it for a better, open-minded understanding. Just because it is a subject matter that is outside of how we were conditioned does not mean that it's evil.

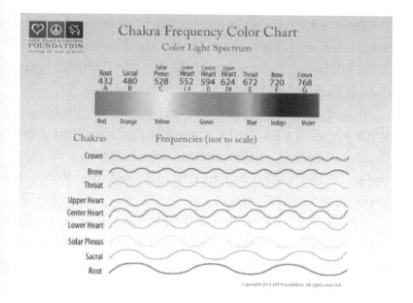

Chakras and musical notes have been paired in many ways. A simple system is to assign sequential notes from the C Major scale to each of the chakras from the root to the crown.

Religious or not, people from all over the world sing and chant. My reason for bringing this to the reader's attention is because of my belief that it's part of our ethereal embodiment, which becomes separated from our present body when we pass away. Bigfoot, being part human, could be tapped into this like us and know better how to use it with their expansive vocal mechanism during their embodiment on this planet. The reader may or may not see the following information about sounds and the Solfeggio chart as interesting as I do, but it can be viewed in its entirety at the Mind Vibrations website.[4]

The Solfeggio frequencies are most commonly associated with the Gregorian chants. The chants are a form of monophonic song of the Roman Catholic faith dating back to the ninth and tenth centuries.

Based on the research of musicologist Professor Willi Appel, it's likely the scale was first introduced by Guido d'Arezzo, a Benedictine monk. Monks of this order of the Catholic Church followed the Rule of Saint Benedict (992–1033).

This scale is the basis for the Do-Re-Mi-Fa-So-La-Ti scale used by vocalists today. So what makes this scale so significant that it's still being talked about and used hundreds of years later?

There's the musical, historical, and religious importance mentioned. These frequencies are also said to have healing attributes. Many people have reported healings when in the presence of Bigfoot. Could they produce the corrective frequency to heal?

Here are the original six Solfeggio frequencies and their said benefits (from the Mind Vibrations website):[5]

- 396 Hz: the first is thought to help liberate us from feelings of guilt and fear, which is arguably one of the biggest obstacles we face in life.
- 417 Hz: the second helps with the undoing of situations and facilitating change in our lives. It is said to alleviate the conscious and

subconscious mind from traumatic past experiences.

- 528 Hz: the third is perhaps the most famous of the frequencies, because of its reputation for creating profound transformation and miracles. It has even been linked to the repair of human DNA, the most basic building blocks of our bodies and minds.
- 639 Hz: the fourth is said to improve our connection and relationships with the people around us. This includes healing strained relationships and creating new ones.
- 741 Hz: the fifth is connected to expression and solutions, helping us open up and share our gifts with the world more fully.
- 852 Hz: the sixth and final of the original notes, returns us to spiritual order, improving our access to the spiritual or sublime.

Many moons ago, I took singing lessons and ran that scale. I also used it a lot when practicing a lead on a guitar, never realizing the significance. This may or may not have much to do with our understanding of Bigfoot, but I thought it was interesting, so I put it in. That said, I have heard a few reports of people who have witnessed a Bigfoot and it turned into a ball of light. Many people claim to have witnessed orbs, too, but many of those same people have been talked out of what they said they saw by skeptics. Our brain has an easier task if its processor was conditioned by something that it has already learned.

I've witnessed orbs at Joe and Tammy Hauser's Montana Vortex and after looking at the picture, saw a complex design within; I suspect that it is a form of energy.

Everything works within a frequency, so if these beings can create a vibrational frequency via octave manipulation with their unique vocal range, it could mean we're getting closer. Some may think that I am stretching this a little, but why not? It gives us more to consider, especially since many people claim to have been healed by these beings.

During the 1890s, Nikola Tesla invented a vibrational sound healing device that was used by Mark Twain. Tesla and Twain were close friends and mutual admirers.[6] But Twain, who was suffering from a variety of distressing and dangerous ailments, agreed to get on Tesla's device. Twain "would continue to use the machine daily for almost two months, at the end of which he had, in the words of Tesla, 'regained his old vigor and ability to enjoy life to the fullest extent.'"[78] Sound healing is becoming increasingly popular.

What about moving things with sound frequency? When that happens, it referred to as acoustical levitation. There are many other interesting anomalies that theorists claim were moved by sound vibration. In the first half of the twentieth century, Edward Leedskalnin formed the Coral Castle in Florida. This reportedly small man of just over five feet tall, who weighed just over one hundred pounds single-handily moved and carved the stones while nobody was watching. How? More on the Coral Castle, megaliths, and levitation in chapter 11.)

All around the planet we find megaliths that were formed by beings with advanced technology. My personal experience was in Peru and Bolivia.

Could those huge boulders, many well over one hundred tons, have been moved with sound technology? If so, what about the way they were put together, like a jigsaw puzzle, with no mortar. An alternative scientific method was mentioned in the previous chapter.

11

LEVITATION

A s we learned earlier, it's been suggested that aliens were the progenitor of Bigfoot, specifically to do the work that the aliens didn't want to do, such as mining gold, heavy lifting, and other hard labor. Most of us have heard about or have seen pictures of the muscular appearance of Bigfoot. Would physical strength alone be the way those hundred-plus-ton boulders were moved in Peru and Egypt? Or could levitation be playing a part?

One evening in 1974 when I witnessed a Bigfoot at the Sierra Camp was the same evening I also recorded the famed "Samurai Cry," and my friend Bill and I actually got glimpses of two of them. The one that I saw was huge, just a silhouette, that streaked through the forest, perhaps fifty yards away, but with a speed and agility that was uncanny. No human that I know of could have run that fast and that smoothly without stumbling or jumping over the deadfall. It seemed to be floating above the ground. I believe that it was a male and was headed toward what we considered to be the female and an adolescent, which I also recorded that same evening with their distinct vocalizations—three separate voices. So, what does this have to do with levitation?

Most who have researched levitation believe that it is accomplished using sound frequency. The being I witnessed seemed to actually be floating above the ground. It was too smooth to be natural. I've wondered if sound frequency was involved.

It's been witnessed and filmed that some monks in the high mountains of Nepal are able to levitate. They chant, and while in a meditative state they are able to levitate above the ground. Records say that some monks are able to rise above the ground up to three feet. It is said that they did not lift off to impress the onlookers; they simply wanted to assume the most suitable position for performing religious rites. Saint Joseph of Cupertino, a seventeenth-century priest who was canonized by the Catholic Church in 1767 by Pope Clement XIII, was reported to have levitated over seventy times by eyewitnesses.[12]

FRA GIOSEPPE DA CVPERTINO DEL ORDINE MINORE DE CONVENTVALI DI S FRANCESCO

Joseph of Cupertino

I am familiar with the illusions that are often used to make this levitation feat appear realistic, but a film I saw on YouTube of a levitating monk in Tibet, did not seem to be an illusion. Plus, there is a history of this happening; not with just one monk, but the levitation of boulders by a group of monks. That too, was filmed, but the film was reportedly confiscated and sealed.

Tibetan monks with horns

Dr. Jarl, a Swedish doctor who had studied at Oxford, made a journey to Tibet in 1939 for the English Scientific Society and filmed an anti-gravity event performed by the Tibetan monks.

Later, the English Society confiscated and classified the two films, refusing to release them.[3]

The ruins of several ancient civilizations—from Stonehenge to the pyramids—show that they used massive stones to construct their monuments. Why?

Could part of the answer be that these ancients had a method of lifting and moving these massive stones—some weighing several tons—that made the task as easy and manageable as lifting a two-pound brick? The ancients, some searchers suggest, may have mastered the art of levitation, through sound frequency or some other obscure method, that allowed them to defy gravity and manipulate massive objects with ease. [. . .]

The fact is, no one really knows for certain exactly how they were constructed. The current estimates of mainstream science contend that it took a workforce of 4,000 to 5,000 men 20 years to build the Great Pyramid using ropes, pulleys, ramps, ingenuity, and brute force. [. . .]

The Egyptian pyramids are not the only ancient structures constructed of huge blocks of stone. Far from it. Great temples and monuments around the world contain stones of incredible size, yet little is known about their means of construction and how they were moved.

The Temple of Jupiter at Baalbek, Lebanon has a foundation that contains the three largest known stone blocks ever used in a man-made structure. Each block is estimated to weigh as much as one thousand tons! No super crane in existence today could lift one, yet they are positioned together with such precision that not even a needle could fit between them. Nearby is an even bigger stone. Known as Hajar al-Hibla—the Stone of the Pregnant Woman—it lies abandoned in its quarry, never used. But the giant rectangular block is thought to be the largest piece of stone ever cut by humans, weighing an incredible 1,200 tons. It is estimated that it would require the strength of sixteen thousand men to even budge it, and it represents a challenge to twentieth century machines and technology.

On an isolated plateau at Tiahuanaco, Bolivia, thirteen thousand feet above sea level, stands an impressive monument called Puerta del Sol, or Sun Gate. The elaborately carved gate weighs an estimated ten tons, and how it arrived at its present location is a mystery. [. . .]

It's remarkable that cultures left no record of how these structures were constructed. However, "in almost every culture where megaliths exist," according to 432:Cosmic Key, (considered the key of the universe and the resonant vibration of all cells in humans). A legend also exists that the huge stones were moved by acoustic means—either by the chanted spells of magicians, by song, by striking with a magic wand or rod (to produce acoustic resonance), or by trumpets, gongs, lyres, cymbals, or whistles.[4]

How unfortunate that these secrets of levitation . . . are lost to antiquity or the remoteness of the Himalayas. They seem to be forever elusive to modern Western man. Or are they?

Beginning in 1920, Edward Leedskalnin, a 5-ft. tall, 100-lb. . . . Latvian immigrant began to build a remarkable structure in Homestead, Florida. Over a 20-year period, Leedskalnin single-handedly builds a home he originally called "Rock Gate

Park," but has since been named Coral Castle. Working in secret—often at night—Leedskalnin was somehow able to quarry, fashion, transport and constructed the impressive edifices and sculptures of his unique home from large blocks of heavy coral rock.

Coral Castle

It's estimated that 1,000-ton coral rocks were used in construction of the walls and towers, and an additional 100 tons of it were carved into furniture and art objects:

• An obelisk he raised weighs 28 tons.

• The wall surrounding Coral Castle stands 8 ft. tall and consists of large blocks each weighing several tons.

•Large stone crescents are perched atop 20-ft.-high walls.

•A 9-ton swinging gate that moves at the touch of a finger guards the eastern wall.

•The largest rock on the property weighs an estimated 35 tons.

•Some stones are twice the weight of the largest blocks in the Great Pyramid at Giza.

All this he did alone and without heavy machinery. No one was ever witness to how Leedskalnin was able to move and lift such enormous objects, although it is claimed that some spying teenagers saw him "float coral blocks through the air like hydrogen balloons."

Leedskalnin was highly secretive about his methods, saying only at one point, "I have discovered the secrets of the pyramids. I have found out how the Egyptians and the ancient builders in Peru, Yucatan, and Asia, with only primitive tools, raised and set in place blocks of stone weighing many tons."

If Leedskalnin had indeed rediscovered the ancient secrets of levitation, he took them with him to his grave.[5]

So, can Bigfoot levitate? My account is only one of many who have reportedly seen a Bigfoot appear to be floating as it moved. We know that many of these giants have a vocal range far exceeding that of humans. Could some make a frequency that could create levitation? From my brief sighting, it moved very fast and smoothly and appeared to have been floating. (And there was no alcohol or drugs involved...just sayin'.)

12

TREES

A few years ago, a man who frequented one of my businesses said that he'd like to talk to me. I'd known this man for years, and what little he ever had to say, most anyone would feel compelled to listen. I was one of them. He was a big man, a muscular, Paul Bunyan type, and quietly lived in the backcountry. He was married to a local Miwok woman. I stopped what I was doing and sat down at his table to listen.

This man knew of my interest in Bigfoot and began to tell me about a sighting he'd had when he was cutting trees on his property. While bucking a log, he noticed, at a distance, what he thought to be a man, squatting down and watching him at the meadow's edge. He knew of no one that was supposed to be in the area, so he immediately put his chainsaw down and began to approach. "Who are you?" he yelled. The being stood up and walked away. While moving away, the entity went behind a large bush. The man said, "It was a Bigfoot." He went to the area and noted that the bush was about seven feet high, but he witnessed the Bigfoot's head a foot over the bush while it was walking away.

This account is like many others that I have heard over the years of people witnessing these giants while cutting trees, especially if the area is being clear-cut. In his book, *The Hunt for Bigfoot* (updated in 2018), the late Peter Byrne interviewed seven loggers.

Peter's book details an encounter that happened on June 22, 2018, when seven loggers working with heavy machinery in the Wilson River watershed area, on the Oregon coast ranges, watched a Bigfoot approach them down through the area above the road. It moved smoothly and rapidly, walked upright with big strides, and then cut away to its right; the short (knee-high) vegetation through which it walked made it clearly visible to the seven men. The time was midday, and the weather was bright and clear.

Trees are very important for humans. Trees contribute to our environment by providing oxygen, improving air quality, improving climate, conserving water, preserving soil, and supporting wildlife. During the process of photosynthesis, trees take in the carbon dioxide that we breathe out and produce the oxygen that we breathe in.

Trees do this for us, and what do we do in return? We cut them down to build our homes; we cut them down for furniture; we cut them down for firewood; and so on. Most of us don't even give it a second thought. We seem to underestimate the value of trees and what they do for us.

There's something about cutting down the forest that seems to obviously disturb these wilderness giants. This is true for many things this earth gives us, and we often take those things for granted.

In Oregon, I met a man who showed me a movie that he took with his camera as he moved through the backwoods on a dusty mountain road. He and his son had been having unusual Bigfoot activity in that area. At the time he took the picture, he was not aware of what he'd captured. Later, from his home, as I watched his film, he pointed out a couple frames where a conical head peered out from a tree but immediately moved back. The head was cone-shaped and did not look human. The other part of that head and the body should have been seen too—so now we have a mystery.

Over my fifty-plus years of researching the Bigfoot phenomenon, I've heard several reports of people claiming that they saw these beings as they disappeared. Can anything disappear? I cover this topic, including cloaking, in more detail in chapter 7. I used to sit those reports on a shelf, but I don't anymore. When several reports from people unrelated to each other are saying the same thing, I think we have to give a certain amount of credence to those reports.

While living in Washington on the Olympic Peninsula, I met a woman who reported that she had seen one of these beings move in, and also out of, a tree. There is also a man, whom I have known for several years who lives in that same state and swears that they move in and out of trees. Native American mythology says that they live in two worlds, that they are spirit beings who can disappear. What do we do with these reports? Indigenous people have been inhabiting this continent much longer than outsiders. So shouldn't we ponder these reports?

In 2018, my good friend, David Paulides, who has written and produced several 411 books and films about missing people, asked if he could go into the Sierra Camp and produce a short film for one of his projects, *Missing 411: The Hunted*. I've known David for many years, know of his integrity, and trust him completely. It is the only professional filming I have ever allowed to visit that camp. The Sierra story received about fifteen minutes of that DVD, but my point is that the few minutes that followed the Sierra Camp clip were directed toward a very credible lady, who witnessed a "predator" type, pixelated image of something that was moving from one tree to another. That same profile fits several reports that I have received. Years ago, at a business meeting in Canada, I first heard something like this. The man knew of my interest in these beings and asked if he could tell me a personal story. He took me aside and said that he could take me to an area northwest of Fairbanks, Alaska, where he saw one of these beings disappear.

Even though this man wore a suit and tie, for a long time thereafter, I put his account on the shelf with other reports that didn't make sense to me. Is it possible that these giants energize inside trees by producing a certain energetic frequency?

Nikola Tesla, along with theoretical physicists, says that at the most minute level of existence, we are energy that vibrates at a frequency. I believe there could be a palpable link between energy, trees, and these big guys. It could also account for new batteries going dead, why we don't see them more often, why they seem to have an attachment to trees, and why they are often reported being seen around power lines. There are many huge trees around the Sierra Camp. Many times, as they vocalized around that camp, I wondered why we didn't see them more often than we did. We could hear a tree pop, but not see anything.

Tree knocking is a very popular thing for researchers to do when they're in the woods. However, to my knowledge, no one has ever seen a Bigfoot hitting a tree. That said, I have recorded the rhythmic tree-rapping sounds. But does that represent, as I've thought, that one was signaling to another, or could it also be something else, something even crazier? A single loud whack might give us another clue. In 2011, when I was at the camp, I heard a very loud tree-knock sound within a few feet of me, but I did not see anything, and it was daylight. Could it have been the sound of their energy leaving the tree?

In 2021, I was privileged to be part of a production

that took place in Portlock, Alaska. It was an eight-part series for Discovery+ and titled *Alaskan Killer Bigfoot*. I was brought there to give advice to the descendants of the people who had been mutilated and/or missing during the late 1940s. They wanted my opinion if it was okay for them to reestablish the village. There was no pressure on me at all. The written history of Portlock is undisputed. After being there for a few days, I truly think there is a mystery lingering in that forest. There was a single tree that stood out among all the other trees that had not been cut many years ago, when there was obviously a lot of timbering going on. It was a very unusual looking tree.

After flying over the area and noticing the heavy timbering from decades earlier, I thought that it may have been one of the problems. If one of these giants came out of the woods and screamed at one of those villagers who was cutting the trees, I have little doubt that the person would have shot it, or at it, and that would definitely have pissed it off.

There were a couple other issues that I brought up, but the subject of trees and showing respect for the area were at the top of my list.

If respect for the land is not shown, I believe it upsets these beings. Trees are a part of their habitat and an important feature of this planet, and that should be significant to us all. They obviously roam this earth and are in harmony with it. We, on the other hand, are always trying to conquer it.

"The earth is a source, not a resource." Chief Arvol Looking Horse, Spiritual Leader of the Lakota

So does that make me a tree-hugger? I really don't want to be placed in that category, but I do love the forest and don't like it being mutilated. And you won't find me out there hugging a tree.

A few years back, a friend who has a home in the Cascades of Oregon claimed that he has a Bigfoot coming around his home. He also gave a sighting report. One day he showed me a tree limb in his yard that was stuck in the ground upside-down. We just don't see that every day. It didn't appear to be a limb that had fallen or blown into his yard. It seemed to have been placed there by something very powerful. In my opinion, it is important to look for all other possibilities before allowing our mystical, conditioned brain to take over. Without an explanation, we have often seen pictures of upside-down trees; most of which are dead. I was queried about that once, but I didn't have a good answer. I just suggested that maybe the tree did not serve a good purpose any longer.

Another theory that has emerged is that the tree is an entrance to the underground. If they energize within a tree, maybe it's a way to return to where they hang out. Is there a more profound *something* that we should consider about trees? Perhaps a spiritual meaning? In ancient writings, the tree is special. In the good book's first chapter of Genesis, we read about the Tree of Life and the Tree of Good and Evil. Is it meant to be taken literally? Or is this allegorically or metaphorically speaking? Trees are mentioned fifty-six times in the Bible and signify many interesting things. So next time you are in the woods and feel compelled to whack a tree, you may want to consider this chapter.

13

AS ABOVE, SO BELOW

Could Bigfoot live underground? Or perhaps be a product of alien intervention into a primates' DNA? Or maybe both? Whichever, we do not seem to be able to find one. Of all the different species on this planet, and this one reportedly so big and also being seen regularly nowadays, why not? That seems to be one of the bigger questions being asked these days. How does Bigfoot stay off science's radar?

According to my research, there are an estimated 8.7 million different species on earth. Of course, nobody has counted them, and no form of data could accurately know that number. Plus, a lot of those species are mostly in our unexplored oceans. The ocean contains 71 percent of the earth's mass, while our land is left with 29 percent.

Our Milky Way galaxy is estimated to have at least

100 billion planets, but "a new study estimates that a mere 300 million of those 100 billion planets may have the right ingredients for life."[1] But who could possibly know what types of environments all forms of life would require? I have noticed that some astrophysicists who study environments on different planets state that a certain planet could not support life, but I say that there's no way they could possibly know. They seem to be comparing other life forms to us and our requirements for life.

Years ago, I hired a new secretary for my office. A lady by every sense of the word, she was very intelligent and she spoke with an English accent; she was great on the phone and would always remind me of important appointments or certain bills that must be paid immediately. However, if a spider began to build a web in the office, she would capture that spider and take it outside; whereas I would have smashed it—I don't like spiders. Why would anyone care that much for an unpleasant creature that builds webs, bites, can hurt, and is ugly? (Well, maybe not ugly to another spider, but certainly to me.) When I was a very young boy, my dad had me drag a wire through a tight crawl space under the house. I couldn't see anything other than a distant light on the other side. However, the spider webs were everywhere, and my face knew it. I think that began my spider phobia.

Many different species are on this planet. Besides the natural evolution of different species, I'm a believer that over eons there have been many interventions by aliens on this planet who have altered the genome of many species. I've wondered if they were put here to hybridize their species into this environment or just to see how we humans would react to those species. Perhaps the earth is just a testing place for many of these different creatures. I think it might be good for us to care about different species that inhabit this planet with us. I have really tried to like spiders, but so far, it's not working very well.

After my last hunting venture years ago, in the Sierra Nevada mountains, while watching a deer's eyes glaze over and its life pass away, I was reminded of when my mother passed away and her eyes glazed over. It made me stop killing things—spiders excluded. It also brought back the idea that perhaps we are supposed to respect, and possibly learn from, different life forms on this planet, including Bigfoot. Many of my good friends still hunt for food; I do not have a problem with that, and I will still eat hamburgers. But hunting just to kill something, however, is a bit of a problem for me. I also have a problem with those who are in the woods to try and harvest a Bigfoot. We humans seem to be a warring species. I think that I've heard about all the excuses for killing a Bigfoot there is to tell. From "We need a specimen for science" to "They need to be protected, so one needs to be brought in" to "They've been bothering my dogs."

I personally don't think it's that easy to hunt or even kill a Bigfoot. Several people have claimed to have shot one and swore they did not miss. That said, when one is in our 3D environment, I think it is probably subject to Newtonian physics and therefore can be shot.

As a young boy, I made a slingshot and would hunt birds. It was fun to see how close I could get to hitting one. But, one day I did. It fell from the tree and when I looked at it, I had peeled its skull and saw its brains. All that bird was doing was singing a song and enjoying its life. So that made me feel bad, and I stopped shooting at birds.

Years ago, I remember reading an interesting book. It suggested how all species on this planet is a type of something that exists in this vast cosmos that we are part of, and it brought to my mind Hermes's Emerald Tablet, with a famous saying (paraphrased) "As above, so below."

One of the most influential seventeenth-century scientists, Isaac Newton, tried to find out the mysterious alchemical text of Emerald Tablet. It is certain that his work was the foundation of classical physics, but one thing most people do not know is that Isaac Newton was also a mystic with a special interest in alchemy.

Emerald Tablet, Translation of Isaac Newton from 1680.

"Tis true without lying, certain & most true. That wch is below is like that wch is above & that wch is above is like yt wch is below to do ye miracles of one only thing."

Emerald Tablet

"The text of the Emerald Tablet, also known as the Smaragdine Tablet or the Tabula Smaragdina, first appears in a number of early medieval Arabic sources, the oldest of which dates to the late eighth or early ninth century. It was translated into Latin several times in the twelfth and thirteenth centuries. Numerous interpretations and commentaries followed."[2]

There's another idea that looms in my Bigfoot wonderment field: What if these giants who we call Bigfoot also exist underground? Possibly with other types of species too? Many think that Bigfoot goes underground and that's why we don't see them more often or find one. After all, some civilizations lived underground centuries ago and perhaps Bigfoot (or

Nephilim or Anunnaki) could still be living there. Following are examples of places that may inspire further exploration of this idea.

Derinkuyu

There's a city in Turkey's Nevesehir Province that was found when a man renovated his house.[3] Upon discovering a secret room during demolition, his explorations led to an "intricate tunnel system with a series of cave rooms. Little did he know it at the time but he had discovered the ancient underground city of Derinkuyu, which was once home to more than 20,000 people and extended to a depth of approximately 279 feet."[4]

Derinkuyu

Göbekli Tepe

"Göbekli Tepe just doesn't make sense. The neolithic archaeological ruins were first uncovered in the '60s, but their significance wasn't truly realized until 1994. The site is located in southeastern Turkey—although it predates the establishment of the country by a significant amount of time. In fact, Göbekli Tepe is so old and complex that it is rewriting our understanding of not just Turkish history, but the entire history of humanity. Based on everything we know about how modern civilization got its start, Göbekli Tepe should not exist, but it does, and has for 12,000 years, possibly much longer.

"Archaeological study of Göbekli Tepe has been going on for a long time—even though the political climate in Turkey has made matters slightly more difficult, some sections are in the process of being restored."[5]

Eridu

Biblical scholars think that Eridu was the original Garden of Eden. It's in southern Mesopotamia (currently Iraq) and may be where humanity began over again with another upgrade by the Sky People (Anunnaki) after the deluge. According to K. Kris Hirst, an anthropologist at the University of Iowa,

"Eridu is one of the earliest permanent settlements in Mesopotamia, and perhaps the world. Located about 14 miles . . . south of the modern city of Nasiriyah in Iraq, and about 12.5 mi . . . south southwest of the ancient Sumerian city of Ur, Eridu was occupied between the 5th and 2nd millennium BCE, with its heyday in the early 4th millennium."[6]

Why is Eridu important in our Bigfoot study? Because I think some of the Anunnaki (Sky People), mentioned in the ancient Sumerian text were aliens who were on earth after the flood. They are depicted to be much larger than humans and were responsible for significant upgrades to humanity. Also, it is possible that Bigfoot may have been on earth prior to the flood but may have survived through one of Noah's daughters-in-law (possibly Ham's wife), who carried a recessive gene, maybe even a recessive giant's gene. To me it seems that it could have left us with a Bigfootlike being as offspring, a diluted hybrid possibly kin to the Edomites, such as pictured in the cave of Michelangelo's painting, The Last Judgment. Those who have looked into this should know that Noah's son, Ham, had a son (Cain) who settled the land known as Canaan where giants lived.

Hang Son Doong Reptilians

Known as the world's largest cave, Hang Son Doong was inadvertently discovered by Vietnam resident Ho

Khanh in 1990. "While hunting in the jungle, Khanh came across the opening. He felt a blast of wind and heard the rush of a river inside."[7] The cave "located near the Laos-Vietnam border opened for tours in 2013 and visitors began to report 'mysterious sightings' of reptile-like humanoid creatures, with at least one person being abducted and never seen again."[8]

According to local residents, the most notable thing about Son Doong Cave is the strange creatures that are believed to dwell within it. They describe seeing reptilian-type humanoid beings emerging from the Son Doong Cave, and they believe that they actually live deep inside this cave.[9]

This underground world has been rumored to exist by US soldiers who told tales of seeing horrific lizard men emerge from it during the Vietnam conflict. The sighting is particularly interesting when put alongside an alleged account that appeared on another website regarding an American military unit that was based in South Vietnam close to the same caves in 1970. The report claimed that a seven-foot "upright lizard humanoid[10] was spotted near the entrance of the cave. The unit eventually opened fire on the creature, but it appeared that it escaped unhurt as no body or signs that it was wounded were found. The anonymous soldier stated that his unit was not debriefed about the incident, which led him to believe that it was either unreported or that it was simply hushed up."[11]

Son Doong

Solomon Islands

Then we have the Solomon Islands, an island country consisting of six major islands and over 900 smaller islands in Oceania, to the east of Papua New Guinea. According to the Cryptid Wiki website, "the capital, Honiara, is located on the island of Guadalcanal. Americans recognize the name Guadalcanal, because of the fierce fighting that took place there during WWII between the Japanese and the Americans. But that was not the only conflict occurring."[12] According to Marius Boirayon, Research Director of the Solomon Anthropological Expedition Trust Board Incorporated, it was reported that the Japanese soldiers encountered a True Giant that was over ten feet tall, with other sightings of "True Giants" reported at more than twenty feet tall.[13]

———

This planet still holds many mysteries, and they are turning up more regularly than ever before. Bigfoot is just one more to be recognized and understood.

What are these giant beings on this planet for? Do they have an agenda? They do not pollute the planet. They do not seem to bother anyone too much, if any. It seems they care more about the earth than most of us humans do. Actually, what animal hurts the earth more than humans? Personally, I think we should take better care of it, not just this planet, but all the life forms that inhabit it with us.

That's just me, however, and there's no offense intended to those who want to save at the grocery store, plant a garden, or hunt for meat to eat; each of us can do what we choose to do and decide what we need to do. On this planet we humans have been given dominion by our creators. Many indigenous people have followed that principal for eons and all of us are supposed to take care of this planet, not damage it. I think it's a shame that humans are a warring species and many want to kill what is not understood and too often what we cannot control.

14

ARTIFICIAL INTELLIGENCE: A WOLF IN SHEEP'S CLOTHING

S cience has now put itself on the dangerous edge with the development of artificial intelligence (AI). From what I am hearing, very soon it will be difficult for us to distinguish the difference between one of them and a human. They will be smarter and more durable than we are. This could get spooky and out of control when AI advances on its own and gains consciousness . . . but is that even possible?

Also, could our awareness, our soul, be transferred into an indestructible body form? It's thought that some very advanced aliens have transferred their consciousness into an indestructible body. Some of the higher-frequency beings do not even need a body. Now wouldn't that be something? However, in my opinion, if we accept that upgrade, we would not be in a position to expand our human evolution and advance to our place in the cosmos naturally; we only evolve through developing our frequency to a higher level through our reaction to experiences, and that's done with our consciousness, which does not die.

My caveat: Since I have written this section on AI, it seems that it has expanded exponentially. It will soon be out of our control. However, it could help humans . . . or not. AI will be producing and programming its own androids anytime, and I don't mean a super-duper cell phone. I think we should all take another look at the ancient text and consider a statement that the master said in the good book. "As it was in the days of Noah, so it will be at the coming of the Son of Man" (Matthew 24:37).

What was happening in the days of Noah? (A world-altering deluge). Aliens (fallen angels, the Anunnaki) were giving advanced knowledge to humans and breeding with human women, creating hybrids and giants. What's happening now? Aliens are here, said to have copulated with human women, and giants are also here. If aliens offered us a body with no pain and we could live a thousand years, wouldn't we be tempted to accept? Be aware that unless the humans that God made are actually what He made in His image and advance via their correct response to their experiences, those humans are stuck in a frequency that would not allow them to advance to the level for which they were intended. The third dimension (3D) is where we are now; 6D is the level of consciousness we need to be to create (many aliens are in the fifth and sixth states), and 9D is the conscious-ness humans are designed for. Could this be what Nikola Tesla meant when he said that to understand the universe, we must understand 3, 6, and 9? (See chapter 6)

We are not at the top of the intellectual food chain. If AI eventually takes control, will they ask, "Why do we need incompetent people?" It's up to humans to show that we represent love and compassion and are worth saving. We are a warring species, and compassion has not been at the top of our list. Most world-power countries are in, ready for, or getting ready for confrontation. If any of them would change that idio-syncrasy, perhaps AI would understand that compassion is a good thing, and we could all work together for a better world.

I believe that most of the world leaders will adopt AI completely and, unless we are aware of this danger, we will all unwittingly become dependent on it.

Could AI be the "Wolf in Sheep's Clothing?" As it is said in Matthew 7:15, "Beware of false prophets, who come to you in sheep's clothing but inwardly are ravenous wolves."

This is, in my opinion, the most important issue facing humans today and is definitely worth considering.

15

AUTHOR'S ADVENTURES AND CONFESSIONS

"We are all born to die. The difference is the intensity with which we choose to live." Gina Lollobrigida, 1927–2023.

Born in June 1942, I have fathered four children: Ronika, Rhonda, Rachelle, and Royce. I'm very proud of them, and glad to be called their father.

Years ago, I was given a birthday card that read on the outside, "You're over the hill now." After I opened it, it read, "You're not just over the hill, but you've passed the valley, gone through the swamp, down the canyon, and headed up the other mountain." But, as with many of us, when my last experience in this body is over, I'll be headed for that white light, long tunnel, or whatever. Possibly I will get hit by a purple wand of enlightenment.

My life has been anything but boring. I have possibly lived a life envied by many. A good friend once called me "The luckiest man in the world." He knew of the many things that have been part of my life, especially the Bigfoot adventures and my many trips to other countries. When I was a young man, I would always venture off, looking for something new. When I reached the age of twenty-nine, in between my Bigfoot undertakings, I kept moving from one adventurous thing to another.

I have been (and still am) a private pilot, and over the years I have owned several airplanes, flown many hours into remote villages of the Alaska bush and south into the jungles of Central America. I've logged several thousands of hours of flying and would generally leave whenever the urge struck me. I was always able to get matters covered with my businesses first, having been very fortunate to have good people who worked for me.

As a SCUBA diver I have ridden on the backs of giant manta rays in the warm waters of Mexico and explored old sunken ships in the cold waters of Alaska. In between these trips I would go hunting or I would explore different parts of the world. But the most exciting was packing the high country in the Sierra mountains of California with my good friend, Bill McDowell. However, as mentioned, I stopped hunting after watching the fading eyes of a deer glaze over and his life leave. I ate the venison, but my then wife wasn't so fond of it. Anyway, I stopped hunting.

For many years I dabbled in music and made two albums. I tested guitars for the Fender guitar company in Southern California, and later I presented my music in different parts of the United States. I also made a circuit flying into the native villages of the Alaska wilderness and enjoyed visiting and presenting my music to the villagers. If I wanted to do something, I figured out a way—neither time nor money would stop me. I was an entrepreneur who owned and successfully operated several restaurants and a motel. At one time I employed over 250 people.

I was also a self-defense instructor who incorporated martial arts into my program. And when I became single, as my last confession, in between wives, I was a womanizer and a misogynistic ass. I objectified women and should have tried to better know who they actually were. For being so superficial and shallow-minded, I sincerely apologize and ask for forgiveness.

Hopefully, I am with the last woman I'll ever be with . . . the perfect one, who I respect very much. She came into my life at a perfect time, a time when I needed to be taught more about many things, including women, and she's still working on me. We mediate, eat right, and breathe correctly. It takes time to clear our minds of the junk that we have been conditioned to believe all our lives and become free to evolve via our own connectivity.

Keri and I live comfortably in the Carolinas. We both have grown children and grandchildren who we are proud of. I lost one daughter, who was much too young to pass, but I have grandchildren that will know things that I won't know during this embodiment. All in all, I am a very fortunate man; I've had excellent health all my life and have now learned to follow the lead of a happily balanced heart.

During my life, with so much of the on-the-edge stuff I have done, I think there's been something, or someone, watching over me—someone whom I've never seen. Decades ago, I could not even imagine that I would be around for the twenty-first century. There must be more for me to answer for, just for more opportunities and experiences to respond to different issues, showing compassion instead of impatience or anger. If we don't learn from history, we're doomed to repeat it. That is what karma is all about. Yes, I can't help but believe in multiple embodiments. It is the only thing that has ever made sense to me. We must get this right to ever evolve into who we were originally designed to be.

Over the years, I have watched high-profile celebrities, many who have passed on now, leaving all their stuff to someone or something. But I also noticed many everyday people become very successful, who had all the toys anyone could ask for. I've been one of those guys. I have done about everything that I've ever wanted to do. However, in my getting-ready-to-leave years, I have found that many of those things that I acquired don't matter now. All I desire now is for my children to have happy, fulfilling lives and to leave something good to be remembered by—something, too, that will help others who were also conditioned in this society, and that's not tangible things. All the stuff that has accumulated means nothing if others who were influenced are left in the dark. I've never saw a U-Haul trailer being pulled by a hearse.

Now that I'm getting closer to the end of this beautiful rainbow, I believe that there's gold there, and here it is: We're all here for life's' experiences, but more importantly, it's how we respond to those experiences. I've come to understand the things that I heard older people say when I was younger, such as "Enjoy life, you only live once." I do not believe that now; I believe we live and learn from many lives.

Older people can get tired from the lack of energy, seeing doctors, and unusual things growing out of our bodies. I promised myself that when I got old, I wouldn't sit around in a coffee shop with other old guys, some of who consider themselves a victim in this life, talking about what medicine I take or the pain I'm in. I say no. No, we should be happy to be old enough to still have experiences' many people seemingly passed much too soon. But who are we to judge when or where someone should pass on? I say, "Who are we to judge anyone's response to their experiences?"

But you know what? There's more to come (energy cannot die), so I am ready for my next adventure, for example being "totally" enlightened and "one" with the universal consciousness. And I want to find my deceased daughter, Rachelle, and see what her energy is doing now.

I've heard it said that money isn't everything, but it sure beats whatever is in second place. I say that second place belongs to money and happiness is in first place. It has also been said that "He who dies with the most toys wins." To all those still hunting for success, unless you're happy, getting more stuff is not the answer. Success is being happy "now." All the toys in the world that we may have accumulated will not go with us. What goes with us is the love and compassion that we have shown to others; it stays with our energy/consciousness part.

And to those aggressive, gun-totin' wood knockers hunting for Bigfoot, I say this: Unless it's a coincidence, you won't find them. However, it is interesting that these unusual giants can find us. And they interact with the ones they want, the ones with the right frequency.

We're all still trying to understand what these giants are, using the best methodology that we think is right. I say keep it up, be influenced by what feels right with your heart (your gut feeling), and remember that we have all been conditioned, so not everything you have been taught is correct.

EPILOGUE

Where do we go from here? It is easy to understand our 3D environment, but we need to conceive the fact that other elements are part of our human construct . . . and those places can be reached during this 3D experience. Without that understanding we cannot achieve the best that is available, and we'll probably need to repeat life in a 3D habitat, somewhere, so we can again have experiences and a chance to graduate (e.g., raise our personal frequency). In this universe, there must be an infinite number of planets in different stages of evolution.

I am relatively sure that different types of beings from the cosmos have been on this planet in the past, and some have probably stayed. Some of them, including Bigfoot, may live underground; some may be a product of a more recent hybridization program;

many could be walking among us unrecognizable, and some could be the creation of someone's overactive imagination. Many researchers are hungry for answers, including me. That said, I know of no person who has researched longer and had the experiences that I have had around these beings, but where did they come from, if they are not just a relic hominid that has escaped classical science? If Bigfoots have an alien component, what alien species were their progenitors? And how many other species have been here and experimented with our evolution?

Eventually everything in this 3D environment must change forms; that's physics. The decisions we've made would determine what happens in our future. We have, and always will have, the freedom of choice.

What if the seeds of life forms came from outside this earth? What if this earth is a type of planet that houses different types of species that at one time actually had their own place somewhere else in the cosmos? Could this be a type of training ground for humans who have consciousness, feelings, etc., and those attributes did not evolve from natural selection? Humans are a special type of hominid and were given dominion on this planet, so we need to take care of it.

The Sumerians from Mesopotamia were responsible for giving the first written language, inspired by the Anunnaki (Sky People). Those clay tablets, numbering in the thousands, are known as the cuneiform tablets—a written account of our history that became the core of many written languages.

It seems obvious that prior to the big deluge, there were hunter/gatherers on this planet. However, we are now discovering that something else was also around then. When we look at Göbekli Tepe and other structures on this planet that were here prior to the flood, it should give us pause.

I think that this concept might give us a better understanding of what humans may be here for. This does not mean that I think evolution did not occur. However, I also believe in intelligent design by advanced high-frequential beings who possibly altered the DNA of different species.

The good book says that we will reign as kings and priests and that humans are special (1 Peter 2:9, Psalms 8, 4–6). Is it really that much of a challenge to be nice, compassionate, and loving to one another? What would we have to lose? We have everything to gain—I suspect the universe. However, it is obvious that humans are a warring species and that we have a lot to learn if we are to keep this beautiful planet.

ADDENDUM 1

THE ANUNNAKI

In 1971, when I first encountered these giants at the Sierra Camp, my quest was to understand just what the others and I were experiencing; a family of gorillas that escaped from another country? Perhaps a zoo? However, my fifty-plus years of looking into this led me to not just Bigfoot, but also the origin of humans.

Having been brought up in religious circles and being a board member of a huge church, I began to search the Bible for answers. Where did giants come from? How are they here now? How are they doing what they do?

Years ago, I wrote an article on the first and second chapter of Genesis; how I thought the two chapters could be representing two different type humans.

In the book of Genesis, we are given a very brief history of the creation of man, how giants came about, a great flood, and so on. However, as my deepening research continued, I discovered that it is believed that all written languages, Hebrew included, have their roots in the ancient cuneiform tablets from Mesopotamia. But who fostered those tablets?

The Anunnaki Star People

The Anunnaki, a group of deities from ancient Mesopotamian cultures, have fascinated historians, archaeologists, and mythologists for centuries. Originating in the Sumerian pantheon, these gods played significant roles in the religious beliefs of the Akkadians, Assyrians, and Babylonians. Known initially as descendants of An, the god of the heavens, and Ki, the earth goddess, the Anunnaki have left an indelible mark on the history and culture of these ancient civilizations.

As the subject of numerous texts and artifacts, the Anunnaki have captivated the imaginations of many, with some even positing that they could be ancient alien invaders from the planet Nibiru. Though these theories remain speculative, the influence of the Anunnaki, particularly in the Epic of Gilgamesh and as inspiration for the deities in later cultures, cannot be denied. The enigmatic nature of these ancient gods promises to keep the intrigue alive and fuel further exploration into the depths of Mesopotamian mythology. [. . .]

The Anunnaki, which translates to "those who

came down from the heavens," are seen as a group of deities from the ancient Sumerians, Akkadians, Assyrians, and Babylonians. According to some beliefs, the Anunnaki arrived on Earth some 432,000 years ago by landing in the Persian Gulf. This advanced civilization is suspected to have played a crucial role in the creation of humans.

The ancient Sumerian texts provide an intriguing account of the Anunnaki's involvement in human origins. According to the myths, they genetically engineered humans by combining their DNA with that of early hominid species in order to create a workforce. This workforce was intended to serve the Anunnaki by mining precious resources and performing various tasks. [. . .]

Some believe that the Anunnaki ruled over the Earth for thousands of years. As mentioned in ancient Mesopotamian texts, these powerful beings had the ability to shape human culture and society. Possessing advanced technology and knowledge, the Anunnaki allegedly bestowed this knowledge upon humans, helping them build impressive structures and establish complex civilizations.

Their rule is believed to have extended to numerous regions, including ancient Sumer, which is considered the cradle of civilization. The Anunnaki's impact on early human societies can be observed in various aspects such as architecture, agriculture, and the establishment of the earliest written language (cuneiform script). [. . .]

As the Anunnaki's history spans over a great length of time, their cultural impact merged with other ancient civilizations, where their legends and beliefs became deeply intertwined with the stories of later cultures, such as the Greeks and Egyptians. Overall, the influence of the Anunnaki across the ancient world demonstrates the powerful and long-lasting impact these deities have had on human civilization throughout history.[1]

ADDENDUM 2
CUNEIFORM TABLETS

Cuneiform can be defined as an ancient writing system used for over a thousand years between various cultures. Cuneiform is one of the earliest writing systems that humans ever developed; it may even be the first one ever. According to Wikipedia:

> Cuneiform is a logo-syllabic script that was used to write several languages of the Ancient Near East. The script was in active use from the early Bronze Age the beginning of the Common Era. Cuneiform scripts in general are marked by and named for the characteristic wedge-shaped impressions which form their signs. Cuneiform is the earliest known writing system and was originally developed to write the Sumerian language of southern Mesopotamia (modern Iraq).
>
> Over the course of its history, cuneiform was

adapted to write a number of languages in addition to Sumerian. Akkadian texts are attested from the 24th century BC onward and make up the bulk of the cuneiform record. Akkadian cuneiform was itself adapted to write the Hittite language in the early second millennium BC. The other languages with significant cuneiform corpora are Eblaite, Elamite, Hurrian, Luwian, and Urartian. The Old Persian and Ugaritic alphabets feature cuneiform-style signs; however, they are unrelated to the cuneiform logo-syllabary proper. The latest known cuneiform tablet dates to 75 AD.

Cuneiform was rediscovered in modern times in the early 17th century with the publication of the trilingual Achaemenid royal inscriptions at Persepolis; these were first deciphered in the early 19th century. The modern study of cuneiform belongs to the ambiguously named field of Assyriology, as the earliest excavations of cuneiform libraries—in the mid-19th century—were in the area of ancient Assyria. An estimated half a million tablets are held in museums across the world, but comparatively few of these are published. The largest collections belong to the British Museum (approx. 130,000 tablets), the Vorderasiatisches Museum Berlin, the Louvre, the Istanbul Archaeology Museums, the National Museum of Iraq, the Yale Babylonian Collection (approx. 40,000 tablets), and Penn Museum.[1]

NOTES

Disclaimer

1. Dr. Lynn Kirlin, Professor of Electrical Engineering, University of Wyoming. In a book by Marjorie Halpin and Michael Ames, *Manlike Monsters on Trial* (Vancouver, BC: UCB Press, 1980).

Introduction

1. Christopher Baird, "Why Do Quantum Effects Only Happen on the Atomic Scale?" Science Questions with Surprising Answers website, April 22, 2014. https://www.wtamu.edu/~cbaird/sq/2014/04/22/why-do-quantum-effects-only-happen-on-the-atomic-scale/
2. Nikola Tesla as quoted on the Goodreads website. https://www.goodreads.com/author/quotes/278.Nikola_Tesla

1. A Misuse of Research

1. Baird, "Why Do Quantum Effects Only Happen on the Atomic Scale?"

2. Body and Soul

1. Albert Einstein as quoted on the Goodreads website. https://goodreads.com/quotes/4455-energy-cannot-be-created-or-destroyed-it-can-only-be

3. Where's the Proof?

1. Later published in a book, *Manlike Monsters on Trial*, by UCB Press, 1980.
2. B. Ann Slate and Al Berry, *Bigfoot* (Toronto: Bantam Books, 1976).
3. Saul Mcleod, PhD. "What Is Cognitive Dissonance Theory?" Updated October 24, 2023. Simply Psychology website, https://www.simplypsychology.org/cognitive-dissonance.html
4. Marjorie M. Halpin and Michael Ames. *Manlike Monsters on Trial: Early Records and Modern Evidence.* Vancouver: UBC Press, 1980.

6. Manifestation Code and Dimensions

1. Matt Williams. "A Universe of 10 Dimensions." December 11, 2014. Phys.org website. https://phys.org/news/2014-12-universe-dimensions.html
2. Nikola Tesla as quoted on the Goodreads website. https://www.goodreads.com/author/quotes/278.Nikola_Tesla
3. Wikipedia, "Third Eye." https://en.wikipedia.org/wiki/Third_eye
4. Andrew Zimmerman Jones. "Biography of Physicist Paul Dirac: The Man Who Discovered Antimatter." Updated December 22, 2017. https://www.thoughtco.com/paul-dirac-2698928
5. Paul Wallis interview with Regina Meredith, "ET Contact and the Bible before God." Found at Regina Meredith's YouTube channel: https://www.youtube.com/watch?v=UreYifdr2fk. Paul Wallis's website is at https://paulanthonywallis.com/

7. Cloaking: Quantum Physics at Work

1. As quoted on the AZ Quotes website: https://www.azquotes.com/author/4399-Albert_Einstein/tag/energy
2. Baird, "Why Do Quantum Effects Only Happen on the Atomic Scale?"
3. David J. Brown. "NASA Discovers Hidden Portals in Earth's Upper Atmosphere." Telescope.com website, June 19, 2013. https://www.telescope.com/NASA-Discovers-Hidden-Portals-in-Earths-Upper-Atmosphere/p/103046.uts

4. Dr. Tony Phillips, "Hidden Portals in Earth's Magnetic Field." Science Daily website. https://www.sciencedaily.com/releases/2012/07/120703140559.htm

8. Intervention and Karma

1. Nikola Tesla as quoted on the Goodreads website. https://www.goodreads.com/author/quotes/278.Nikola_Tesla

9. Hybridization

1. Salama Yusuf, "Why Can't Mules Have Babies?" *Springfield Sun* website. November 30, 2020. https://www.scienceabc.com/nature/animals/why-cant-mules-have-babies.html
2. Kevin Leroy Harter, "Does Mitochondrial Introgression Explain the Sasquatch Genome Project Data Better than a Human Hybrid of Recent Origin?" *Relict Hominoid Inquiry* 10:77-112 (2021). https://www.isu.edu/media/libraries/rhi/essays/HARTER-FINAL.pdf
3. Dr. Francis Collins, *The Language of God: A Scientist Presents Evidence for Belief* (London: Simon & Schuster, 2008).
4. Wikipedia, "Göbekli Tepe." https://en.wikipedia.org/wiki/Göbekli_Tepe
5. Jon Austin, "DNA Tests Reveal Where 'Elongated Heads Came From,'" February 13, 2018, ExoNews website. https://exonews.org/dna-tests-reveal-where-elongated-heads-came-from/
6. April Holloway, "Ancient Humans Bred with Completely Unknown Species." November 13, 2013. Ancient Origins website, https://www.ancient-origins.net/news-evolution-human-origins/ancient-humans-bred-completely-unknown-species-001059
7. McKenzie Prillaman "These Shape-Shifting Devices Melt and Re-Form Thanks to Magnetic Fields: Gallium Plus Magnetism Equals Something Straight Out of *Terminator*." January 25, 2023. https://www.sciencenews.org/article/robot-shape-shifting-gallium-melt-reform-magnetic-fields

10. Light and Sound

1. Borel, Brooke. "Sound Becomes Light." March 19, 2009. Popular Science website, https://www.popsci.com/scitech/article/2009-03/sound-becomes-light/
2. Admin, "Difference Between Light and Sound." July 8, 2011. DifferenceBetween.com website. https://www.differencebetween.com/difference-between-light-and-vs-sound/
3. Johannes Van Zijl, "This Is How Sound Is Turned into Light." February 1, 2016. The Science Explorer website, http://thescienceexplorer.com/universe/how-sound-turned-light
4. Mind Vibrations, "About Solfeggio Frequencies," n.d. https://www.mindvibrations.com/solfeggio-frequencies/
5. Ibid.
6. Ian Harvey, "The Wacky Friendship between Mark Twain and Nikola Tesla." From the Vintage News website, January 11, 2019. https://www.thevintagenews.com/2019/01/11/twain-and-tesla/
7. The complete story of the Tesla/Twain healing can be viewed at: https://universe-inside-you.com/nikola-teslas-vibrational-healing-device-sound-vibrational-medicine/
8. Universe Inside You website, "Nikola Tesla's Vibrational Healing Device: Sound & Vibrational Medicine." https://universe-inside-you.com/nikola-teslas-vibrational-healing-device-sound-vibrational-medicine/

11. Levitation

1. More can be found about this historical figure at https://www.youtube.com/watch?v=gb7RSMMTg7U
2. Catholic Online, "St. Joseph of Cupertino." December 6, 2019. On YouTube at https://www.youtube.com/watch?v=gb7RSMMTg7U
3. Ellie Crystal, "Tibetan Sound Levitation of Large Stones Witnessed by Scientist." Ellie Crystal's Metaphysical and Science website. https://cdn.preterhuman.net/texts/other/crystalinks/levitationtibet.html
4. Steven Wagner, "The Ancient Secrets of Levitation." Updated on February 17, 2019. LiveAbout website. https://www.liveabout.

com/the-ancient-secrets-of-levitation-2593647
5. Ibid.

13. As Above, So Below

1. Passant Rabie, "Scientists Pinpoint How Many Planets in the Milky Way Could Host Life." October 30, 2020, Inverse website. https://www.inverse.com/science/how-many-planets-host-life
2. Wikipedia, "Emerald Tablet." https://en.wikipedia.org/wiki/Emerald_Tablet
3. Wikipedia, "Derinkuyu Underground City." https://en.wiki pedia.org/wiki/Derinkuyu_underground_city
4. Jackson Groves, "Derinkuyu Underground City in Cappadocia, Turkey: Visitors Guide." June 24, 2023, Journey Era website. https://www.journeyera.com/derinkuyu-underground-city-cappadocia
5. Stephan Roget, "This Archaeological Site Is Rewriting Our Entire Understanding of Human History." Updated August 21, 2021, Ranker.com website. https://www.ranker.com/list/facts-about-gobekli-tepe-turkish-archaeological-site/stephanroget
6. K. Kris Hirst, "Eridu (Iraq): The Earliest City in Mesopotamia and the World." Updated on March 10, 2019, ThoughtCo. Website. https://www.thoughtco.com/eridu-iraq-earliest-city-in-mesopotamia-170802
7. Kate Springer. "World's Biggest Cave Is Even Bigger than We Thought," Updated May 19, 2019, CNN website, https://www.cnn.com/travel/article/son-doong-cave-vietnam-expedition/index.html
8. Lon Strickler, "Vietnam: Recent & Wartime Reptilian Cave Encounters," February 7, 2015, Phantoms & Monsters website. https://www.phantomsandmonsters.com/2015/02/vietnam-recent-wartime-reptilian-cave.html
9. Ibid.
10. Vicky Verma. "Gigantic Underground Cave in Vietnam Could Be Habitat to Ancient Reptilian Race," April 5, 2023, Hows and Whys website. https://www.howandwhys.com/vietnam-gigan tic-underground-cave-habitat-to-ancient-reptilian-race/
11. Ibid.

12. Cryptid Wiki, "Solomon Island Giants." https://cryptidz. fandom.com/wiki/Solomon_Island_Giants

13. Ibid.

Addendum 1

1. Annunaki.org, "The Annunaki: Ancient Sumerian Gods and Their Legacy on Earth," https://www.annunaki.org/

Addendum 2

1. Wikipedia, "Cuneiform." https://en.m.wikipedia.org/wiki/ Cuneiform

For Ron's books and downloads, please visit www.ronmorehead.com/products. For additional products visit www.thebigfootstore.com.

Made in United States
Troutdale, OR
05/29/2024

20220248R00106